**Gelong Thubten** is a Buddhist monk, meditation teacher and author from the UK. After studying at Oxford University he embarked on a career as an actor but suffered severe burnout. This led him to join Kagyu Samye Ling Tibetan Buddhist Monastery in Scotland, where he became a monk in 1993.

Gelong means 'fully ordained monk', and Thubten's training has included spending over six years in intensive meditation retreats, the longest of which lasted four years. He has studied under some of the greatest Tibetan meditation masters.

Thubten is a pioneer in meditation and mindfulness teaching, with over 20 years' experience working in schools, universities, the NHS, companies, prisons and addiction counselling centres. He designs meditation courses for medical students and has lectured at Oxford

University. He also works with major organisations such as Google and the United Nations, and he is regarded today as one of the UK's most influential meditation teachers.

Thubten's first book, *A Monk's Guide to Happiness* (Yellow Kite, 2019) was a *Sunday Times* top 10 bestseller and has been published in more than 15 countries worldwide, including the US. In addition, he and neuroscientist Dr Ash Ranpura collaborated with Ruby Wax on her bestselling book and tour *How to be Human: The Manual*.

Through his writing and work, Thubten supports charities that establish meditation centres to benefit local communities. He has set up a number of such outreach projects, bringing meditation teachings to some of the most deprived areas of the UK.

Thubten is also a trustee of ROKPA International, the humanitarian aid charity established by his teacher Akong Rinpoche and Lea Wyler, with projects focusing on education, healthcare and the environment in Tibet, Nepal, Zimbabwe and South Africa.

Dedicated to Akong Rinpoche,
Lama Yeshe and my parents

# HANDBOOK
# FOR HARD TIMES

Also by Gelong Thubten

*A Monk's Guide to Happiness*

# HANDBOOK
# FOR HARD TIMES

## A MONK'S GUIDE TO FEARLESS LIVING

## GELONG THUBTEN

First published in Great Britain in 2023 by Yellow Kite
An imprint of Hodder & Stoughton
An Hachette UK company

The authorised representative in the EEA is Hachette Ireland, 8 Castlecourt Centre, Dublin 15, D15 XTP3, Ireland (email: info@hbgi.ie)

7

A CIP catalogue record for this title is available from the British Library

Hardback ISBN 978 1 529 36765 2
ebook ISBN 978 1 529 37063 8

Typeset in Celeste by
Palimpsest Book Production Ltd, Falkirk, Stirlingshire

Printed and bound in Great Britain by Clays Ltd, Elcograf S.p.A.

Hodder & Stoughton policy is to use papers that are natural, renewable and recyclable products and made from wood grown in sustainable forests. The logging and manufacturing processes are expected to conform to the environmental regulations of the country of origin.

Yellow Kite
Hodder & Stoughton Ltd
Carmelite House
50 Victoria Embankment
London EC4Y ODZ

www.yellowkitebooks.co.uk

# Contents

# CHAPTER 1
# HARD TIMES

**'Pain is inevitable, suffering is optional.'**
**HARUKI MURAKAMI**

Early in the morning of 8th October 2013, I woke to shocking news. I was told that Akong Tulku Rinpoche – my spiritual teacher, mentor and closest friend of more than 20 years – had been brutally murdered.

At the time, Rinpoche was in Chengdu, China, about to embark on his annual visit to his homeland of Tibet. We had been speaking by phone every day, and between our last communication the night before and this particular morning, he had been killed in a most horrible manner. A gang of three men burst into his apartment and Rinpoche, his nephew and his attendant were stabbed to death. They were attacked for the money Rinpoche was about to distribute to the orphanages and hospitals he had established through his charitable organisation. The perpetrators were quickly found and imprisoned by the police.

Details soon emerged. It turned out that we knew the main assailant – he was a Tibetan friend of ours who had previously spent some time at our monastery in Scotland. He had been a devoted monk, but it seems that after returning to Tibet, he had developed a psychotic illness. He was the most violent of the attackers, stabbing Rinpoche in a vicious frenzy.

I could hardly believe what I was hearing, and felt completely distraught. Rinpoche was a hugely important figure in my life, so this was an inconceivable loss. We had a long history: soon after I had arrived at the monastery as a troubled 21-year-old, he had taken me under his wing and helped me find my feet. A few years later, I became his assistant and we would travel on teaching tours, working closely together for several months every year. He taught me everything I know about meditation and guided me in my work. I saw him as both my teacher and my dearest friend. His sudden death was a profound tragedy for the Buddhist world at large, and for me, it felt as if my entire universe had come crashing down.

Akong Rinpoche was loved and respected by many. He

was a highly regarded spiritual leader, yet would always be the quietest and most unassuming person in the room. He was instrumental in introducing Buddhism to the West, and established the Samye Ling Monastery in Scotland, where I am a monk. Despite his role, one would often find him in the monastery grounds cleaning out drains with his bare hands or tidying up after others, always an example of humility.

He was also a skilled physician and celebrated humanitarian, responsible for hundreds of projects in some of the world's most destitute regions, where he had set up orphanages, schools, hospitals and soup kitchens for the homeless. He was known for his great kindness, immense wisdom and deep sensitivity to the suffering of others.

When I got the news, I was in Oxford visiting relatives, and my first reaction was to fall into paralysing shock – my body became like stone and my mind froze. I then went into emergency mode, highly focused, contacting the relevant people and trying to deal with the unfolding crisis. I had to keep silencing my emotions by pushing them to the bottom of my mind. Fear would arise and I would slam the door on it, not ready to face any of the dark feelings that were coming up in me.

In times of trauma, a person will often use forceful

suppression as a means of survival, and I knew this was the only way I could keep going. Later that morning, as I realised the enormity of what had happened, I began to experience strong panic attacks. My body would shake and I found it impossible to speak or weep, even though hot tears were building up and fighting for release. Then the phone would ring, putting me straight back into work mode. I was oscillating between falling apart and operating at high levels of efficiency.

Having been Rinpoche's assistant for many years, I was now one of the people thrown into the middle of handling legal matters as well as fielding questions from the media. It was helpful to keep busy, and while prayers and ceremonies were taking place at the monastery in Scotland, I went to our London branch to deal with administrative issues and complex communications. I would spend my time pacing the corridors while making incredibly difficult calls, including figuring out how we could get Rinpoche's body back from China.

As the days went on, I began to feel an unusual strength emanating from deep within my body, pushing me forwards and making me highly focused. At night, however, I would fall into grief and a visceral sense of fear. Losing Rinpoche made me feel like something within me had been savagely torn, and I also wondered if we were all under attack and who might be next. I would lie in bed unable to sleep, feeling the heat of pain and terror, as if my entire body was in flames.

News began to filter back to the UK. I had to study the police report, which described with precision the vast number of stab wounds, and I found myself involved in the complicated process of helping to retrieve Rinpoche's belongings. My good friend Lea, who had also worked closely with Rinpoche for many years, flew out to Chengdu and phoned me from the flat where the murder had taken place. She was hunting for his things while I helped her remember what to look for. She said the place was completely soaked in blood. To this day, I have no idea how she was able to handle such an experience.

After much negotiation, we managed to get Rinpoche's body transported to his monastery inside Tibet for cremation. Because of my responsibilities, I had to remain in London, continuing with the press interviews and other tasks. I kept replaying the horrific images in my mind, searching for answers. In addition to feeling an immense sense of loss, I could not fathom how such a deeply spiritual, selfless and compassionate person as Akong Rinpoche could have met this dreadful, violent end. It was also terribly sad and shocking that two other people had been killed with him. Every day, however, that curious mixture of sadness and strength continued to emerge, as if something was slowly growing in me to nourish and sustain my mind.

The nights were a very different story, as my distress took over. I realised I needed to tap into what I had learned some years earlier, during a four-year-long meditation retreat in which I had struggled with extreme depression. Fighting the suffering had just made it worse, whereas embracing it with acceptance turned out to be immensely transformative. Now, as I lay in bed, I knew to slip into a space in the middle of my feelings without pushing them away. I understood that letting go of resistance and moving closer would stop the pain from destroying me. This softened its edges and made it feel significantly more manageable.

The members of our Buddhist community around the world were in shock, but nobody seemed angry – there was a level of forgiveness amongst all the grief. It felt natural not to fall into feelings of vengeance. Many of these people had spent years practising compassion meditation, and now the results were evident: there was a profound sense of loss but no hint of rage or any wish for revenge.

We wrote petitions to the authorities in China requesting that the killers be granted reprieve from the death penalty. Of course, we all agreed that they should remain in prison because they were dangerous people, but to hate them and wish for them to be killed because *they* had killed felt inhuman. Our plea was not upheld, and at the time of writing, nine years later, the perpetrators are still on 'death row' somewhere in China.

Some of my strongest memories of Rinpoche are of the times when he would speak about the power of acceptance and compassion. None of us wants to suffer, but when it does happen, we have no choice but to find a way through it. It turns out there is much we can learn from the hardest of situations, and Rinpoche would often say that the fastest way to grow is through facing up to our pain, rather than shying away from it.

## A HANDBOOK FOR HARD TIMES

We have instruction manuals for many things in life, but when we encounter hard times, we often lack guidance and have very little idea of what to do. Our main desire is just to escape as quickly as possible, but we soon discover that when we run from our feelings, our problems simply become worse.

My first book was called *A Monk's Guide to Happiness*,

and after completing it, I decided to write about how to work with difficulties, or, as my publisher joked, 'a monk's guide to misery'. I wanted to explore how a richer, more sustainable happiness can emerge from the transformation of suffering, and how our *unhappiness* is the most fertile ground for the cultivation of inner strength, resilience and compassion.

We humans have built rockets to the moon and are now able to send telescopes beyond our solar system, but we find it hard to deal with what goes on inside our own heads and hearts. We seem to have evolved externally but not internally, looking outwards but not inwards. We seek happiness but rarely do we understand that to find it, we must transform our minds. We wish to avoid suffering, but seldom do we realise that the solution is to change how we think.

The message of this book is that hard times are a useful opportunity – if we know what to do with them. We have a strong habit of pushing away discomfort and chasing its opposite, with the result that we usually find challenging situations intolerable. The key to sustainable happiness is to be found in learning how to handle adversity.

Even when facing the most difficult events of our lives, nothing will ever truly destroy us if we learn how to transform our minds and work *with* instead of against our problems. There are some key principles in Buddhist philosophy which can help with this.

## THE NATURE OF SUFFERING

The Buddhist approach begins by exploring the question, are we ever truly happy, or is there always something holding us back? We are all familiar with obvious pain and stress, but are we not also driven by an ongoing, hidden sense of suffering that keeps us trapped in a cycle of constantly grasping at or rejecting things? Our first step is to take a closer look at this.

Perhaps the word itself, 'suffering', is a problem. It is too blunt a term for describing a whole set of feelings ranging from mild irritation to extreme trauma. Buddhist books can at first be a little off-putting, as 'suffering' seems to appear on every page (as it does in this book!). One might be left thinking of Buddhism as being somewhat heavy and depressing. Of course, when Buddha taught, he didn't use that word. It is a modern translation of something far more subtle, called *dukkha*. This also covers discomfort, dissatisfaction, uncertainty and vulnerability – basically, the human condition.

Buddhist teachings go into much detail examining the nature of *dukkha*, so that we come to know what we're dealing with and how best to work with it. Sometimes we go through extremely hard times where it feels as if everything is falling apart, but *dukkha* also points to a fundamental insecurity that bubbles away beneath the surface of our lives, even when things appear to be going well. That insecurity colours pretty much everything we do and how we think. When we acknowledge and understand it, we can begin to find solutions.

The undercurrent of *dukkha* seems to pervade our very cells. Alone and without distractions, we might notice a sense of unease, frustration and incompleteness lurking in the shadows of our minds, often coupled with physical tension. Clearly, nobody wants such feelings, but we don't really know what to do with them, and so tend to keep ourselves busy in the hope that they will go away. Buddhist philosophy describes the *pervasive* nature of our suffering and suggests that until we properly transform our minds, we will never truly get what we want.

## AN ENDLESS SEARCH FOR HAPPINESS

There is something in our attitude that doesn't add up. We strive to be happy but are never sure how to get there. We don't seem to realise that a lot of our suffering comes from how we go about seeking its opposite. There is a certain amount of societal pressure at play here – we are constantly told we *should* be happy and that there's something wrong with us if we're not, but we remain unsure of what that happiness *is*. It feels elusive and depends on many unpredictable factors.

We would all like to experience pleasant feelings, which we mistakenly think of as end-products given to us by the events, objects and people in the world around us. Consequently, we feel a sense of failure when we don't get what we want, or encounter what we don't like, but do we ever really know what it is we are looking for?

We long to possess the things we think will make us happy, only to discover that even after obtaining them, our desires have not been fulfilled. This means we never seem to achieve anything, as even when we do, we find ourselves still hoping for more or looking for something else. We feel perpetually unsatisfied, caught up in a continual chase.

Ultimately, it is the *search* for happiness that makes

us suffer. Searching leads to *more* searching, without any end. Additionally, in telling ourselves we want happiness, we are focusing on a *lack* of happiness and cultivating feelings of discontent, with a need to keep hunting for what we think is missing.

In pushing away discomfort, we usually don't see how the discomfort lies in the pushing. It is our *habit* of chasing pleasure and running away from hardship that is the real problem, as any habit simply proliferates – so we constantly chase more and push away more, reinforcing our sense of dissatisfaction.

Meditation paves the way for changing those tendencies so that we can work with challenging situations and cultivate the crucial skills of gratitude, compassion and forgiveness. This book is intended to help you progress far beyond the basics of your meditation practice: a handbook to support you in hard times, but also to serve as an ongoing resource for *all* times. The methods are not something only to dip into when you're feeling off-kilter, but are designed to be practised regularly. If you can weave them into your life, they will make you more resilient and better able to handle whatever difficulties come your way.

## THE PATH TO TRANSFORMATION

The approach presented in this book may at first seem counterintuitive – to *lean in* to our suffering – but it is highly effective. If we learn to stay with our painful feelings without running away, we can dissolve our resistance and how we experience difficulties will begin to change. It is perfectly normal to go through hard times, but how we *react* is everything, showing us that, as quoted at the start of this chapter, 'pain is inevitable, suffering is optional'.

Meditation has now entered the mainstream. Much of today's popular 'mindfulness' movement focuses on calming the mind and reducing stress, but at a certain point, people can wonder 'what's next?' Many of us long to go deeper, to fully understand our true nature and to bring a greater level of peace and happiness to the world around us. We are looking for a path that will completely transform us.

Amongst the Buddhist teachings, there are lesser-known, powerful techniques that *use* pain and suffering to deepen our meditation practice, awaken our compassion and cultivate wisdom. Traditionally, such teachings were not made public, but it seems that now is a time when our world needs them the most, and so the aim of this book is to share some of those methods.

## BUDDHISM

This has not been written exclusively for the Buddhist reader, but there are some important aspects of Buddhist philosophy and meditation which can be profoundly helpful for those who wish to gain a better understanding of themselves.

What *is* Buddhism, anyway? It is neither an 'ism' nor a belief system, but simply a set of methods to help us explore the nature of consciousness and transform how we suffer. Historically, there was no such word as 'Buddhism'. It was a term coined by 19th-century Western scholars to describe teachings that were starting to spread to the West. In the traditional languages of Sanskrit and Tibetan, one finds names such as *dharma*, meaning 'reality', or *nang rigpa*, which means 'the inner science'. These are significant terms – the practices rely less on belief systems and more on techniques that help us question our fixed ideas about reality, which means investigating how our minds perceive that reality. The methods require us to turn our attention *within* to connect with our capacity for awareness and to awaken our innate compassion. Buddhism is less a religion than a science of the mind, a journey of inner work leading to insight.

## THE LOTUS IN THE MUD

You will fall in love with your life when you can embrace the darkness as well as the light. Initially, this might sound challenging, but meditation helps you get there, reframing hard times as opportunities. That transformation is symbolised in Buddhist art by the lotus, which is a beautiful flower that usually grows in muddy, swampy water, a reminder that happiness can emerge where you would least expect to find it.

It is the most difficult events that can help you to grow. To get there, you will need a road map to fearlessness, a path with clear steps to follow. Meditation, when done with the right attitude, provides that guidance. This book will help you deepen your practice by showing you how to work creatively with difficult situations, giving you greater strength as you learn to bring whatever happens to you onto your path. The aim is for you to make friends with everything in your life, including whatever hurts.

I feel I have made peace with Rinpoche's death, which is what I believe he would have wanted. The experience was terrible at the time, but it has made me more resilient and taught me how freedom can be found even in the darkest places. I am not suggesting we should bypass our suffering or that it's 'all in the mind' and we can simply get over it. I am proposing that if we go deeper into our unhappiness we will find a secret doorway to a power hidden deep within us.

My wish is for this book to help you walk through that doorway. If you learn to meditate, your pain can be felt but will not destroy you. In fact, it can help you grow in ways you never imagined possible.

## MEDITATION EXERCISE: PREPARATION

Every chapter will end with a meditation technique, each building on the last, providing you with a step-by-step path. Those of you familiar with meditation might recognise the first couple of exercises, which are essential groundwork for the more advanced practices that follow.

The first exercise prepares your mind for further meditation, helping you become ready to go deeper as the book progresses. It involves turning your normally outward-facing attention around so that its focus is directed inwards.

• • •

Sit in a comfortable position in a relatively quiet place where you won't be disturbed.

Bring your mind into connection with your body. Quite often, your body is here in the room but not your mind, which is busy with distracting thoughts of the past or future. Here, you are teaching yourself to be fully present.

Become aware of the contact between your body and the chair. Feel the chair under you and behind your spine. Spend a few moments exploring the sensations involved in sitting.

Then, feel the ground under your feet (there is no need to take off your shoes).

Next, pay attention to your hands, which are resting in your lap or on your legs. Notice the texture of your clothing, and how that feels under your fingers and palms. Try not to *think* about it too much, but instead just experience the sensation of contact.

Turn your attention to your shoulders and notice how any stress and tension fall away as you bring your focus to that area.

Now you are going to move further inwards. Become aware of your mind and observe the flow of thoughts. Notice if you feel busy or groggy and sleepy. In either case, simply be aware, without trying to make your mind do anything, without even trying to meditate.

Spend a few minutes just being with yourself in this way, and then end the session by relaxing in your chair, with your mind at ease and without any sense of pressure or a need to achieve anything.

# CHAPTER 2
# FEARLESS LIVING

**'True fearlessness is not the reduction of fear,
but going beyond fear.'**

**CHÖGYAM TRUNGPA**

Before I became a monk, I would go to wild parties that started at 3am in dark, underground clubs with their walls painted black and extremely loud music. I lived in London and then New York, first as a musician and then an actor. I was young and trying to 'make it', convinced I was fearless and thinking I was having a great time.

My family had broken up in my teenage years when my parents painfully divorced, and after university I went into acting. I was beginning to suffer from depression, but threw myself wholeheartedly into a party lifestyle, running from my suffering by trying to get out of my head. I also thought that if I could stand on a stage and get an audience to love me, I would be happy. Much of my behaviour came from a place of fear – looking back, I can see that I was driven by an almost constant anxiety and the fear of being alone. I was afraid of myself.

After moving to New York to further my career, things unravelled and I became seriously unwell: the depression and anxiety, combined with an overload of stress and addictions, all contributed to a sudden and frightening heart problem that stopped me in my tracks. I was unable to get out of bed for several months, with palpitations and panic attacks, my mind consumed by a pernicious sense of dread. The doctors told me it was extreme burnout. I thought I was dying.

My mother, who was also living in the United States at the time, took care of me while I was sick. I devoured the books on meditation I found in her room, drawing comfort and inspiration from their pages. At the same time, an old friend told me about a Tibetan Buddhist monastery in Scotland that had recently opened its doors to people who wanted to become monks and nuns for a year. This deeply resonated with me: my life was in shreds and I needed to do something radical to rescue myself. The books I was reading were telling me that we are more than our pain and suffering, and that we *all* have the potential for transformation. I knew I had to do something about my mind. I was drawn to the idea of taking a year out from life to learn meditation and get myself well again. When my health grew a little stronger, I made the journey to Scotland.

Samye Ling Monastery is a remarkably beautiful place, situated in the gentle hills and forests of the Scottish borders. It takes you by surprise: as you drive through the typical local countryside, the golden roof of a Tibetan temple suddenly emerges from the trees. It is the oldest and largest Buddhist monastery in the West, with a thriving community of monks, nuns and laypeople. It is known for its authentic, traditional teachings and commitment to helping people regardless of their faith or background.

I was surprised by what I found there. I had been expecting to see pious-looking monks with a misty look in their eyes, but instead encountered an eclectic bunch of earthy, kind, open-hearted people who knew what it is to suffer and were now searching for deeper meaning in their lives. Some of them had incredibly colourful pasts, which made me feel very much at home. I had discovered my 'tribe', and less than a week after arriving, I became a novice monk. It didn't feel like I had joined a religion, but more a secret laboratory for the mind.

I quickly settled into monastery life. Our daily programme began with early-morning meditation, followed by some simple work to help with the running of the place. My first job was to make beds and clean rooms in the guest house. The afternoons and evenings were spent studying Buddhist philosophy and practising more meditation. We took the monastic vows to be celibate and to abstain from harming others, stealing, telling lies or taking intoxicants.

I managed to keep to the vows but was by no means a model student, often missing sessions or hanging out with my new friends instead of studying. However, I was getting more and more interested in everything I was learning about Buddhism, and slowly my sense of commitment began to deepen. I could feel something pulling me further in.

Despite this, I was still plagued by debilitating amounts of fear. I experienced an almost constant anxiety which would sometimes spike, making me quite terrified. My heart was still unstable and would beat too fast. This was more than just a case of being too worried: my previous 'wild' lifestyle, combined with trauma from painful events in my teenage years, had been quite damaging. I would feel uneasy and uncomfortable in myself, as if my body and mind were my worst enemies. I would look for *any* possible distractions so I wouldn't have to sit with my thoughts.

I felt supported, however, by the community spirit I found at the monastery, with like-minded people on a shared journey. I quickly discovered the nourishing warmth of spiritual friendships. It was also there that I met my teacher, Akong Rinpoche, who introduced me to the rich wisdom of Buddhist philosophy and began to instruct me in meditation. For the first time in years, I felt safe and inspired.

As the months went on, I started to regain my health and to feel less tormented by unhappiness. I could see how chasing my desires and a fear of my own emotions had kept me trapped for so long. I was beginning to understand the meaning of inner, rather than 'outer', happiness and to become less dominated by anxious thoughts. I wanted to go deeper and began to feel that being a monk for just one year was perhaps not enough.

## A CULTURE OF FEAR

As I reflect on those early days at the monastery and remember that incredibly frightened young man, I often think about where we are right now in our culture. Back then, I had my own experiences of living with anxiety, but it seems that today, we *all* experience a whole new level of societal fear.

Our collective consciousness is now tuned in to a sense of danger at the global level, something we are constantly reminded of by the 24-hour news cycle. We live against a backdrop of pressing existentialist threats, such as pandemics, wars and climate change, all of which tap into our basic instinct for survival. This is profoundly exacerbated by the frantic pace of our lives and our immersion in technology.

We may have achieved a greater degree of material comfort, but it has come with rising levels of unhappiness and dissatisfaction. Life for many is now dominated by stress, coupled with an ongoing search for relief, as we inhabit a culture that continually triggers our fears, creating internal and external tension as we rush from one thing to the next. This can spark an overload of the stress hormones cortisol and adrenaline in our bodies, both of which lead to worry and exhaustion. Our days are filled with a sense of increasing speed, and our minds, just like our lives, have become far too busy.

Fear can affect *any* of our life experiences. Even the feeling of happiness itself is often tinged with some sort of uneasiness. We now tend to *chase* happiness through short bursts of pleasure, looking for a quick fix or a 'high', always seeking out the next 'hit'. Our manner of consuming media, information, experiences, even food, tends to be about grabbing bite-sized morsels of excitement and lurching from one 'buzz' to the next. Searching for pleasure in this addictive manner just leaves us more dissatisfied and fearful of not getting what we want. The wanting mind quickly reaches for more, while feeling empty inside, something cleverly exploited by our consumer culture. If a person worries that they won't get something, they will work harder to obtain it. This is often how things are sold to us, through the constant manipulation of our fears.

We seem to have become more fragile than ever, sensitive to tiny amounts of discomfort. We are so obsessed with feeling good that we have become less resilient, afraid that the smallest thing might upset us, even the tiniest change in room temperature. Again, this is exacerbated by the barrage of online imagery presenting so-called perfection to which we are encouraged to aspire.

Modern life, particularly in urban settings, requires us to cope with pressure that often tips into an atmosphere of threat as we are repeatedly reminded of risks and dangers. When we board a train, for example, one of the first things we hear over the loudspeakers is, 'If you see something suspicious, phone this number.' Over and again, we are told that something dangerous could happen at any moment, spiking our latent fears. Whenever I arrive at a venue to give a talk, I am immediately shown what to do if the place goes up in flames. Of course we need to be safety-conscious, but surely this is not a relaxing way to live.

As we all know, things took an alarming turn in 2020, when the coronavirus pandemic spread across the world. We were confronted by our deep-seated need for survival as the daily news informed us of death tolls, with constant reminders of peril. We grew particularly afraid for our vulnerable and elderly friends and relatives. We encountered fears we had simply never felt before. To walk down a street and feel nervous that the people around us might be vectors of infection, or to worry that a parcel delivery could have bits of Covid on its packaging, and to wonder if we should be washing our shopping, all indicated a new level of all-pervasive anxiety. It felt like being at war with an invisible enemy that was hiding, but absolutely everywhere.

## FEAR OVERLOAD

There is no doubt that technology has brought immense benefits to our world. There is, however, a troubling downside in terms of its effect on our minds. We can use meditation as a powerful way to protect ourselves, but first we need to identify the nature of the problem.

The main issue is our unnatural relationship with information – it now comes *to us* in a persistent and heavily filtered manner. Newsreaders and reporters use a dramatic and alarming tone of voice, putting their audience on edge. The news instantly arrives on our phones, every day punctuated by 'breaking' alerts conveyed with urgency and a sense of panic. The *invasive* nature of this information delivery can play havoc with our nerves.

Our media is now heavily monetised. We are almost helplessly drawn into reading an online piece through an arresting, often fear-inducing headline. Then, we open the article to find it embedded with advertisements, a process commonly known as 'clickbait'. Our anxiety levels are being manipulated for financial gain, making it harder for us to trust the things we read.

A new type of fear has come into our lives with the growth of social media: the worry of not having enough 'likes'. Are we sharing things online out of a sense of generosity and the wish to inspire others, or is there a constant need for validation? We have an experience, we photograph it, perhaps applying a filter to make it look more appealing, and then post it online to see if other people 'like' our lives. We seem to have forgotten how to know if we are enjoying ourselves – we feel we should put our experiences out there to check if other people will confirm that we are having fun. Only then can we be sure we are happy. We have empowered our 'friends' (and how many of them do we actually know?) to make decisions about our happiness. The level of anxiety provoked by social media has become an alarmingly serious problem among young people, in some cases contributing to mental illness and even suicide.

Fear has always influenced the world of politics, but it seems to have become the major ingredient in many a campaign playbook over the last ten years. We are now discovering just how much technology can influence the acquisition of votes, and how culture wars are stirred up though 'filter bubbles', where previous online behaviour informs algorithms of what to serve up on our screens. Many a vote has been won by tapping into a population's implicit bias and tribalistic tendencies. Persuasive technologies have made it easier to control people by manipulating their anxiety levels, getting them to think their way of life is at risk and that their countries might be taken over by strangers.

Consumer culture is another area where fear dominates. We *expect* our surroundings to provide us with happiness – our socio-economic system persuades us that satisfaction comes from external objects, and we feel anxious that we won't have enough. The messaging has become more insistent than ever as it fills up our devices. We are *required* to feel dissatisfied, which makes us keep striving for more – if we are told that something is missing from our lives, we will go after it. Our ancient, deeply ingrained hunter-gatherer instinct means we are genetically programmed to worry about scarcity, and so we pay attention when we are urged to 'hurry up and buy while stocks last'.

## HOPE AND FEAR

Buddhist philosophy describes the mind states of hope and fear as key factors in the psychology of suffering. In this context, hope does not refer to a positive attitude, but instead an expectation that something or someone will come along to make us feel better. We seem to live between those two polarities – *hope* that the world around us will give us happiness and *fear* that it might not.

This has become pervasive, affecting so many aspects of our daily lives, even down to how we use our phones, which have become little devices of hope and fear carried around in pockets and handbags. They trigger a sense of hope that something interesting will pop up to entertain us, or a fear that we might miss out on something or be confronted by bad news. Those moments of hope and fear throughout our day can make us obsessively grab our phones to check – what's happening, what are we missing? A lot of work goes on in the background to keep the fires of hope and fear burning. As we scroll through our social media feeds, the companies behind those technologies have scattered rewards into our screens, a trail of breadcrumbs leading to an elusive 'prize'.

Such a frenetic lifestyle stimulates our 'reptilian brain', the area connected to our survival instinct, stoking a visceral sense of anxiety: the 'fight-or-flight' response, even at a very subtle level – but there is no fighting or fleeing for us, as we remain caught in a loop. Clearly, the effects on our mental health are concerning.

This challenging climate is ideal for meditation. Buddhism is a 2,500-year-old tradition that retains its relevance because its teachings focus on the nature of the mind and how to train our thoughts and emotions. The techniques don't need updating – they are timeless.

The details of life will naturally vary during different historical periods, but what remains constant is how our minds get stuck in patterns of thinking, feeling and reacting, and how that makes us suffer. The 'technology' of thought is beyond history or culture: suffering is suffering, whatever century one lives in.

## FEARLESS LIVING

I have always been a somewhat fearful person, so to write a book with the rather lofty subtitle 'a monk's guide to fearless living' feels like a bit of a stretch. I think, however, that my experiences of working with my fears over the years have given me something meaningful to share here.

To be fearless is not simply about being unafraid. Genuine fearlessness comes from a thorough under-standing of fear. It is by *leaning in* to our fear that we can attain greater stability and strength, cultivated through patiently working on our minds.

Fear has the potential to teach us. Instead of allowing it to trigger our usual set of reactions, we can turn towards the fear and let it introduce us to fearlessness. Facing up to ourselves, with compassion, is an act of courage. A lot of what we do is an attempt at escaping from our feelings.

In that sense, we are always on the run, but to stop running and become comfortable with those emotions is to be brave. We can learn to *face* our fear, not in the usual sense of conquering the things we are afraid of, but by looking directly at the essence of fear itself.

Our meditation enables us to do this, as we turn our normally outward-focused attention within and recognise the feelings of fear. It is important not to buy in to the 'stories' that our minds tell us, but instead to rest our awareness *on*, or even *in*, the fear. This revolutionary method transforms our meditation into an expression of true fearlessness. A fuller explanation, with step-by-step instructions, will be found later in this book.

It is fear which opens the door to that discovery, and therefore it has a *purpose*, reminding us to reconnect with our power. Whenever we are afraid, we can be grateful that our bodies and minds are trying to wake us up to our potential.

We would all like to become more fearless, and practising meditation helps us build mental strength as we gain a better command of our thoughts and emotions. Strength is developed through pressure, and our suffering *is* that pressure. The solution lies within the problem – hard times help us build resilience, the fearlessness required for a life of genuine freedom and happiness.

Training our minds through meditation gives us the tools for achieving that transformation in attitude, and if we know how to meet our suffering in the right way, the problems themselves will make us stronger. Again, to gain strength, we need to encounter something heavy – we wouldn't go to the gym to lift feathers.

## FEARLESS MINDFULNESS

A key ingredient in fearless living is the practice of being mindful. This teaches us to stay present and unconditionally embrace every experience, which is the essence of fearlessness. We are learning to stop running from the uncomfortable, knowing that our discomfort only comes from resistance.

In Buddhist terminology, mindfulness refers to bringing our attention into the here and now, both during meditation and in repeated moments throughout the day.

Initially, it can be quite hard to commit to sitting down regularly to meditate – there is often a degree of resistance. In that case, a more gradual approach would be to start by training in short periods of mindfulness during ordinary activities. As we grow familiar with the feeling of being mindful, we can gain the confidence to go deeper into more formal practice.

'Micro-moments' of mindfulness can be practised even during busy times by bringing our attention into the present, just for a few seconds. We live in a culture of digital 'snacks', where we feel compelled to keep checking our phones throughout the day, overloading our brains and increasing our anxiety, but this can be remedied through short bursts of mindfulness – a very different type of snack.

The opposite of fear is trust, and mindfulness helps us fully trust whatever is happening right now. We can drop our judgements, our usual complaining internal monologue, and instead rely on the fact that everything 'is what it is' – which means we can experience our lives with kindness and wisdom.

Trusting in this moment means to give up our battle with reality – that constant wish for a situation to be different. This does not imply passive acceptance, but a brave ability to take things as they come. It is the *only* way to find happiness.

## MEDITATION EXERCISE:
## MINDFUL MOMENTS

The easiest approach is to use your body as the focus, by feeling the ground under your feet, or, if seated, by paying attention to the sense of contact between your body and the chair, for short periods of time. As you wash your hands, for example, you can feel the soap, the water and your hands rubbing together under the tap. As you clean your teeth, you can focus on the sensation of the brush against your mouth, and the taste of the toothpaste.

You could begin by choosing a couple of actions that you do quite often, and designate them as hooks on which to hang your mindfulness practice. Those actions become mindfulness 'triggers', and a habit starts to build over time. Later, you can expand your mindfulness to other situations, so that it becomes a repeated experience scattered throughout your day. Through this, you are learning to trust in the present moment, which is a key element in the journey to fearlessness.

Next, you can deepen your mindfulness by applying it to challenging situations, starting with small steps. Standing in a queue or being stuck in traffic become opportunities for training in dropping resistance. Usually, in those situations, you might grow impatient and frustrated, but you can teach yourself to stay with the moment, without judging or pushing it away. You are stuck there anyway, so you might as well make the best of it.

Any type of waiting is particularly fertile ground, as when we are waiting, we tend to meet our edge – we grow tense, wanting the situation to change, because we don't like it. It is highly beneficial to practise mindfulness at these times. You might start by becoming aware of your body and its contact with its surroundings. It is easiest to direct your focus to bodily sensations, creating a gentle training in acceptance, being okay with what is.

Become aware of your shoulders or your hands. Bring your attention to your body and relax into the stillness inside you. Feel the ground beneath your feet, or the seat under you.

You might tense up again, but just keep relaxing, being mentally present and using your body as the anchor.

This exercise helps you to drop resistance and see the waiting situation – the difficult moment – as a gift, an opportunity. Without the queue or the traffic jam, how else could you develop this useful skill? When you have decided that waiting is good for you, it helps you establish neural pathways of unconditional joy, as you look forward to the next traffic jam as a chance to do some training. That is how neuroplasticity works: whatever you do repeatedly becomes who you are.

Every time you are in a queue feeling irritated, you are moulding yourself into becoming a more irritable person. If, instead, you can teach yourself to remain positive in that moment, you are building the habit of independent happiness – learning to feel joy against all odds. Your relationship with the things you find uncomfortable begins to transform. By staying with discomfort without running away, you become powerful.

# CHAPTER 3
# MEDITATION

**'Don't just do something, sit there.'**
THÍCH NẤHT HẠNH

The first time I tried meditation, I hated it. I had just become a monk and sat down in the meditation hall at my monastery. All I could think of was how on earth was I going to clear my mind, and how long would I have to sit there for. I remember staring at a pillar in the large, brightly painted room, feeling tense and a little bit queasy. My entire session was taken up in thinking how bad I was at it.

I persisted every day. After a few weeks, I began to experience a sinking feeling in my chest, a sort of sadness or disappointment. This worried me. When I discussed it with Rinpoche, he seemed to know exactly what was going on. He told me I was meditating like an addict, using it like a drug, looking for a high. At first, I was a little taken aback, but then realised he was right – I *had* been trying to get a 'buzz' from my meditation, sitting and waiting for it to make me feel good. *That* was why I felt such a heavy sense of disappointment – desire always leads to more desire and a feeling that something is missing. I needed to learn to practise with less expectation and less attachment to outcomes.

Despite these insights, I was becoming more tense in my meditation. I was locked in an internal battle of fighting my thoughts and feelings, assuming I had to get rid of them and become tranquil, like a still lake. I thought the aim was to clear my mind, which I found both impossible and stressful. Although I longed for peace and quiet, an escape from the inner storm, I was worried I might lose my personality and become like an automaton, a sort of 'Stepford monk'. However, I would look at my teachers at the monastery, and they certainly had character and were not robots. They seemed so utterly *free*, full of joy and compassion. I wanted to be like that.

Rinpoche carefully began to teach me that meditation is not about going blank or 'switching off'. Our ideas of wanting to 'clear' or 'still' our minds are misleading and simply create more stress for ourselves. Thoughts and emotions are not to be discarded but to be worked with, as *fuel* for our practice and as friends rather than foes.

## WORKING WITH THOUGHTS

I now discover that my misconceptions about clearing my mind are quite common, causing trouble for many people when they try to meditate. The more we attempt to silence our thoughts, the louder they will shout, making us want to run away from our session and do just about anything else. The *only* way to sustain a regular practice is to learn how to stop fighting ourselves.

In terms of practical steps, our first task is to learn how to manage those thoughts. Initially, it is helpful to have something to focus on. The mind is hungry, so offer it some food – a meditation 'object'. We might choose to focus on our bodies, our breathing or any of the senses. These all have one element in common – they give us somewhere to come back to from distraction.

The most well-known technique is the use of breath as the 'object'. This involves sitting still for a set period of time – for a beginner, a session might last 10 or 15 minutes – and to practise focusing on the flow of the breath, without trying to control it. Our attention will wander, which is completely normal and not a sign of failure. The point of the exercise is simply to keep coming back to our breath, with gentleness and precision, and without judging our thoughts as 'good' or 'bad'.

From the perspective of neuroscience, the part of the brain that relates to 'rumination' or mental chatter, and the part connected to experiencing our senses are known as 'competing' brain networks. This means they cannot both be active at the same time. Normally, we are able to perform many types of multitasking, such as driving a car and talking with our passenger or walking while listening to music. Crucially, however, we cannot be caught up in thinking while being aware of our breathing or another sense – it can only be one or the other.

It is the *coming back* to the breath that builds our strength, and by challenging our habit of 'jumping' into our thoughts, we gain more authority over our minds. Eventually that power can expand into our lives, reducing the hold our thoughts, and also our emotions, have over us. There is nothing inherently 'wrong' with them – and, as already mentioned, they don't need to be removed – but it is important to get fully into the driving seat and have greater choice in terms of how we think and feel. In our meditation, every time we return to the breath, we are 'becoming our own boss'. Also, the cultivation of a non-judgemental attitude towards our thoughts and feelings is of key importance, which means we are learning to be happy *no matter what*. We will only find genuine happiness when we learn to embrace the present moment 'just as it is'.

## THREE PHASES OF MEDITATION

As we get started, our meditation session will involve three phases that are constantly repeated. The first is when we are 'with' the breath, the second is the moment of noticing our distraction and the third is when we are returning to the breath. Each of these phases has value – they are *all* meditation. Being with the breath is when our attention is 'riding' the breath, as if on a horse – we are staying with our breathing, being aware of it, feeling it and focusing on it. Then, we get caught up in thoughts, emotions, memories, bodily sensations, noises from outside – anything. This is normal, and doesn't mean we have failed. In fact, it is the precursor to the second phase, which is to notice that we have been lost in thoughts instead of following our breath. There is no need to tense up and feel we've made a mistake. This is another important aspect of our meditation – we have regained our awareness, and can now gently return to the breath, which is phase three.

If you understand that these phases – breathing, noticing and returning – *are all* meditation, your practice will become revolutionised. You will realise you no longer need to feel like a failure when your mind wanders. If 'returning' is one of the phases that makes you strong, you need to have somewhere to return *from*, so the thoughts that took you away are precisely what allow you to come back. They *help* the meditation.

## FREEDOM

Meditation is a journey to freedom, a concept we all value highly. Throughout history, people have fought hard and endured great sacrifices in the name of freedom, a fight which continues in many places. I think it is also crucial to explore this at the inner level. We all have a pressing need to free our own minds.

The expression 'a free mind' usually refers to an

independent, free-thinking person who has their own views and is not controlled by others. Buddhist philosophy points to a deeper, more internal interpretation of freedom. We may be strong, intelligent people, making our own choices, but are our minds truly free?

Our thoughts and feelings often go to places we would rather they didn't. We also find it hard to stay focused and keep our attention where we want it. We don't appear to be fully in charge of ourselves. We impulsively react to situations, and our habits and moods often seem to run the show. Do we *ever* really make our own choices, or are those choices subtly controlled by habits and conditioning? To what extent are we simply reacting to life rather than responding? If we are doing, saying and feeling things but later regretting them, perhaps we are not as free as we thought.

## STAYING WITH DISCOMFORT

Meditation helps us discover the real meaning of freedom, but it is not always a comfortable process. It involves a certain amount of work and determination. In monasteries, we sit cross-legged on the floor, which may not be the easiest posture, but it is very helpful for our practice.

One particular benefit is that it transforms our habit of resistance. We feel some discomfort, and rather than getting up or moving, we learn to stay with it, challenging our tendency to run away from difficulties. Of course, no one should cause damage to their body, but to put up with minor aches and pains, as well as a sense of restlessness, is an important part of the training. When we stop looking for comfort, our meditation can take us to a deeper level.

Today, many people prefer to meditate on chairs, which still has benefits. Even on a chair, we have to 'stay' when we feel fidgety and want to get up to move about. That 'staying' is a powerful form of compassion – we are refusing to give up on ourselves. To remain when we want to run away – because sitting still is bringing up resistance – is deeply transformative.

Outside of our session, those little moments of stress that we experience throughout the day, such as waiting for things and feeling impatient, become helpful opportunities for our training in dropping resistance. Normally, we get frustrated, but instead we can use mindful awareness to help us stay with the moment instead of judging or pushing it away.

Without doing this type of work, we may grow increasingly sensitive, irritated by just about everything

– it is always too hot, too cold, too boring, too 'this' or too 'that'. We inhabit a world that keeps promising us endless pleasure, and we go through life constantly reinforcing our habits of wanting to get comfortable and to avoid discomfort. When we approach old age, and everything becomes more challenging, we usually meet our lack of resilience. However, it is never too late to learn meditation, which can teach us to be happy in every situation.

When we turn meditation into a daily habit, it gives us the space to respond to life with clarity and compassion. As we discover how to step back and observe our minds, we won't get so caught up in our own internal whirlpool. Then, we will become less driven by negative thoughts and better able to cultivate positive ones.

I am often asked, 'How can I use this to deal with a crisis?' or 'What can I do when I am really stressed?' These questions suggest there might be a shortcut, a magic button to press when we hit trouble, but actually it is all about the preparation. If we are not practising regularly, there is less we can do in the heat of the moment. In a crisis, our habits of reactivity take over, and any notions of being mindful tend to fly out of the window – we just react. We cannot simply keep meditation up our sleeves ready for emergencies, but we can establish a habit of daily practice, arming ourselves with the strength required for handling life's difficulties. Our training can then 'kick in' when we need it the most.

## THE PSYCHOLOGY OF THE MIND

We have now understood that we are not trying to clear our minds. Our work is in transforming how we relate to our thoughts, emotions and habits. When we meditate, we begin to see our psychological patterns more clearly. We might wonder if we should be exploring some of that 'content', to understand and try to resolve it, but the approach in meditation is more about looking at *how*, rather than *why*, we suffer.

Attempting to find solutions within the content can create even more material, with an endless process of searching. Instead, we could explore how our minds latch on to painful thoughts or feelings and become glued to them. Then, we can learn to undo that habit of grasping. We are investigating the functioning of the mind itself and reprogramming how it deals with its thoughts and emotions.

It doesn't really matter, then, what comes up in our meditation – all that counts is what we are *doing* with whatever arises. The content is *never* as important as the nature of the mind itself.

## A MEDITATION SESSION

It is important to set aside some time every day for your practice. As you carve out those moments for yourself, you don't need to feel guilty for not being busy doing other things – remember that what you are about to do will help you to transform your life at a deeper level.

It is crucial to set a timer for your session – if you sit down and just 'see how it goes', then your practice will become dictated by your moods and never really progress. It is far more effective to commit to sitting for a set length of time. You might begin with ten minutes each day, preferably first thing in the morning, building up to longer sessions as the weeks and months go by. If it's hard to find time in the mornings, you could try later in the day or evenings. What is most important is to practise daily, but not always necessarily at the same time.

Whether you are sitting on the floor or a chair, good posture is important as it balances the mind and enhances your meditation. The main point is to have a straight back, if possible. Sitting up straight encourages alertness and the generation of awareness. It is important to remember that you are doing this to wake up, rather than to fall asleep!

It is good to leave your eyes open. Many people are tempted to close their eyes, but that can lead to sleepiness or a sluggish and unaware state of mind. Having your eyes open enhances mental clarity and vibrancy. It is also helpful to remember that meditation is not about closing down or shutting out the world, but the development of fearlessness. You are here in this moment, awake and fully present, rather than blocking anything out. Non-judgemental awareness means to leave things as they are. Closing your eyes means you are somehow judging the world around you, seeing it as a problem for your meditation. It is better just to leave your eyes open, without trying to change anything.

Natural background noise is fine – it is almost impossible to find a completely quiet place, and it is good to learn to accept whatever sounds arise. It is not beneficial to use special music as an aid, as that can become a crutch, making it harder for you to integrate your practice into your daily life. Again, the idea is to be present with this moment, just as it is, in its natural state, without alteration.

## MEDITATION EXERCISE: BREATHING

The first formal exercise is a seven-step breathing meditation, which is the foundation for all further practices.

Set a gentle alarm or have a clock nearby, so that you can time a 10- or 15-minute session. As you become more familiar with meditating, you could begin to lengthen your sessions.

**1.** Find a quiet place and sit on a chair, with your back straight. It can be helpful to place a small cushion behind the base of your spine for lower-back support, but it is better not to lean against the back of the chair unless you have physical difficulties and need to do so. Your feet are placed in parallel, flat on the floor.

Rest your hands in your lap with the right hand on top of the left, palms facing upwards and the thumbs gently touching. Alternatively, you can place your hands, with the palms facing down, on your knees or resting on your thighs.

Slightly lengthen the back of your neck by gently tucking in your chin. Let the tip of your tongue lightly touch the roof of your mouth, just behind the top row of teeth. Your lips and teeth are neither clenched shut nor hanging open – there is a little bit of space between them.

It is good to keep your eyes open, with your gaze softened, angled slightly downwards but without letting your head lean forwards. You're not looking around the room or at anything in particular, but instead gazing into the space in front of you. Remember to blink whenever you need to. It can be tempting to close your eyes, but this tends either to promote sleepiness or reduces your mental clarity.

Breathe through your nose if you can, otherwise through your mouth. Try not to alter your breathing – just let it remain natural.

**2.** Mentally set an intention of kindness. Spend a few moments cultivating the motivation to practise meditation for everyone's benefit as well as your own. As you progress on your journey, your ability to help yourself and others to find liberation from the deeper causes of suffering will develop and grow, and here you are planting those seeds of compassion.

**3.** Now focus on the feeling of the ground under your feet, and then the contact between your body and the chair. Shift your focus to the texture of your clothing under your hands. Next, become aware of your shoulders, and lastly bring your attention down to the front of your body, your abdomen. Spend a few moments on each of these areas.

**4.** Notice how your breath moves your body with a subtle sense of contraction and expansion. You might feel this in your abdomen or your chest. Remember to breathe naturally and without effort, not trying to breathe deeply but just allowing things to be as they are.

When you realise your mind has wandered, gently come back to your breath, again and again.

**5.** This is the main step, so spend the majority of your session here. Bring your focus to your face, feeling where the air comes in and out, again breathing normally. If you can breathe through your nose, focus on the air as it travels in and out. You can feel the air lightly brushing across the skin at the edge of your nostrils. If it is easier to breathe through your mouth, focus on your lower lip, sensing how the air moves across that area.

Your mind will easily get distracted, which shows just how addicted we all are to thinking. It is ultimately *why* we suffer – we get overly caught up in our minds. Simply return to your breath, with patience and gentleness.

**6.** To end your session, perhaps after 10 or 15 minutes, focus again on your body for a few moments. Feel its contact with the chair, and then the ground under your feet.

**7.** The last step is another moment of compassion, again reminding yourself that you are practising meditation for your own benefit and also for others. You are training in developing greater kindness towards yourself and everyone else, as a path to complete freedom.

# CHAPTER 4
# EMOTIONS

**'The ocean is never bothered by its own waves.'**
**AKONG RINPOCHE**

Towards the end of my first year at the monastery, I decided to continue for longer – something in me was beginning to change. I took vows for another year. Some of my friends were taking lifelong vows, but I felt conflicted. I found the idea of remaining a monk for my entire life both compelling and preposterous, telling myself I had joined a monastery to get a heart condition fixed, with a 'real' life to go back to, and that I was not 'monk material'.

My mind would go back and forth between resistance and inspiration. I would alternate between wanting to pack my bags and leave, or taking on the most difficult, impossible tasks I could think of. In my second year, for example, I locked myself away in a nine-month solitary meditation retreat which involved long periods of fasting.

A retreat takes place in a secluded environment, with at least 12 hours of meditation each day and no contact with the outside world. To some people, the word 'retreat' might sound like a spa break, a relaxing time to unwind and switch off. A long retreat could even seem like running away from life and not facing up to things. I discovered quite the opposite, as all distractions are taken away and we are left face-to-face with our own minds. There is no more running away.

The retreat was not easy. I would sit there, day after day, with turbulent emotions rushing through my mind. I discovered just how much I disliked myself. I had always grappled with a harsh inner critic, a habit of self-loathing, and as the retreat went on, that voice became amplified, as if it was shouting in my head. Today, I find it has lost its power and I simply don't hear it anymore, but during that retreat the internal monologue of self-disgust became loud and oppressive. At the same time, my trust in the power of meditation was beginning to deepen.

I could see that I had been given powerful tools for transforming my mind. I found it reassuring that I was never told to suppress or abandon my emotions, but to look at them with honesty and to work with them. This approach felt healthy and correct, but the work was messy and difficult. I persisted, knowing it was what I needed and feeling grateful for the opportunity.

After the nine months of retreat were completed, there was a shift in my resistance and the idea of becoming a monk for life no longer seemed so crazy or impossible. I began to consider it seriously. I realised that to give up because of finding things too hard was not a reason to leave. I wanted to stay and continue, to deepen my practice and conquer my fears. I was beginning to see the benefits of a life dedicated to meditating and discovering the path to compassion. I found it challenging, but felt a deep conviction that it would not only help me, but also give me a way of helping others.

Soon after that first retreat, I decided to fully commit, and I took lifelong monk's vows. Now, at the time of writing, I have been a monk for 30 years and can honestly say it was the best and happiest decision that I ever made. I have never been someone people would think of as a monk 'type', but I remember after the ordination ceremony feeling every cell in my body click into place, as if I had come home.

## MEDITATION AND THE EMOTIONS

Some common misconceptions aimed at Buddhism are that we are not allowed to feel anything, our emotions are bad for us and the goal is to get rid of them, almost as if to become dead inside. Many people tell me they feel drawn to the Buddhist path but are concerned about giving up their sense of passion and having to erase their feelings.

This is not the case at all. Buddhism is not 'against' the emotions, but it introduces us to something deeper which lies beneath them – our inner potential for unconditional joy and happiness, our capacity for genuine freedom. Buddhism views the emotions as being like waves, coming from a deep and rich ocean.

Every day, we experience a multitude of pleasant and unpleasant emotions. It is obvious that the painful ones destroy our peace of mind, but even the pleasant ones can bring us problems. We tend to define our happiness as when we are feeling positive emotions, but this is ultimately unreliable, as those emotions are usually sparked by external triggers, all of which are changeable and unpredictable. As our lives go up and down, so do our emotions, leaving us perpetually unsettled.

Meditation helps us become less dependent on the things around us to make us feel good, and less agitated by negative situations. Our positive emotions are fine in and of themselves, but we easily become addicted to them, wanting more and feeling dissatisfied. We also get attached to those external triggers, firmly believing we *need* them for our happiness. We become afraid of losing them and ending up unhappy.

We usually settle for a 'conditional' type of happiness, where we think we can only feel good in pleasant situations. Conventionally, if someone feels delighted without any tangible cause, they might be considered a bit odd. Happiness for no reason makes little sense to us, as we tend to believe there must always be a justification. This attitude, however, puts us in a vulnerable position, as it means we can only be happy when the circumstances are right.

Additionally, much of our energy goes into fighting our painful emotions. We long to get rid of them, but that approach never seems to work. The aim of meditation is *not* to eradicate our emotions but to harness their power. By facing them directly and transforming how we relate to them, the 'power' lies in their ability to unlock our capacity for acceptance – and acceptance is our key to finding sustainable happiness. The first step on this journey is to develop a clearer understanding of what those emotions *are*.

*The Merriam-Webster Dictionary* defines an emotion as: 'a conscious mental reaction (such as anger or fear) subjectively experienced as strong feeling usually directed toward a specific object and typically accompanied by physiological and behavioural changes in the body'. The Buddhist definition goes further, describing emotions as 'obscurations' or 'veils', which suggests they are not the complete story but conceal or block something deeper.

The emotions hide our true nature, like clouds obscuring the sky. No matter how many clouds there are, the vast sky behind them remains unaffected. Similarly, our awareness is 'bigger' than our emotions and, like the sky, remains unspoilt by any disturbance that occurs within it.

What is obscured is our innate perfection, like a jewel covered by mud. That jewel is our 'Buddha mind': our potential for true inner happiness and freedom. The mud represents the obscurations – our emotions and fixed beliefs about ourselves and the world around us. As our practice of meditation starts to wash away the mud, our jewel, which is our source of natural unconditional joy, can begin to shine. To get there, we first need to understand what blocks us, so it is helpful to get to know the mechanics of our emotions.

Emotions are with us all the time as latent habits or tendencies which arise as feelings when we are under pressure. We constantly carry the capacity for anger, for example, but we only *feel* it when we are provoked. In that moment, we are never quite sure what to do – the more we 'get into' it, blame it on others, express it, or try to push it down and suppress it, the stronger it seems to grow in the long term, and the more trouble it creates in our lives.

One of the Buddhist terms for emotions is 'inner afflictions', which indicates that when we suffer, we are being afflicted from *within*, not, as we might think, by something external. Of course, an event may trigger us, but it is our feelings which then take over, and *they* are where the suffering comes from.

Rarely do we understand this crucial point. When we feel angry, for example, we usually assume the suffering has been inflicted on us by others – somebody did something and now we are upset. On the surface, this appears to make sense, but a closer examination shows we can only feel anger if we already have the potential for it. Without possessing that seed, the *habit* of anger, no matter how much we are pushed, it will not arise. Perhaps we might instead realise that the other person is in pain and deserves our compassion. Maybe someone pushed our buttons – but a button, of the mechanical kind, works by having a coiled spring behind it. What has been stirred up is our latent anger, our own particular coiled spring. The key word here is *our* anger. There may *seem* to be an external event, but the emotion occurs within our minds, which is where we can find the power to transform it.

According to Buddhist philosophy, no matter how complex we might appear, we only really have three emotions: fear, desire and anger. Other feelings, such as jealousy, hurt and sadness, are simply combinations of fear, desire and anger. We experience all three, but in each of us, one is usually the strongest, our 'leading habit'.

## FEAR

Fear manifests as terror and worry, or an undercurrent of uncertainty that can even pervade an entire culture. Fear is often felt as an uncontrollable churning or fluttering sensation in our bodies. We might detect an uncomfortable hole somewhere deep in the pit of the stomach, or a subtle and unsteady internal 'current' that feels almost like an electrical fault. Fear comes from the anxiety of not knowing: we don't know what might or might not happen, which makes us afraid, stirring up frightening possibilities. Fear tends to be focused on the future, even when that is only a split second away.

If we are a fear 'type', we feel tight with anxiety, our worldview shrinks and we may even become like an animal with its herd mentality, blindly following conventions. Fear prevents us from knowing how we really feel

– we become afraid to look within and lack emotional intelligence. We often suppress our feelings, which can be detrimental to our health and happiness. Fear makes us uncertain of how best to help ourselves, causing us to look for happiness in places where it cannot be found. As if stumbling in darkness, we can go through life without much self-awareness or ability to make healthy choices.

In general, a fearful mind either panics, filled with anxious and upsetting thoughts, or it goes to the other extreme and mentally shuts down, becoming blank and heavy. We fall into a state of emotional 'blackout', where there is no mental clarity or focus.

If our main affliction is fear, we are more likely to experience a cascade of thoughts when we meditate. We can easily slip into rumination or feeling dull, heavy and sleepy. We tend to get *lost* in our thoughts and emotions, with very little control. None of this is ultimately a problem, as if we keep going, our meditation will put us in touch with our awareness, which can never be busy, sleepy or afraid.

To a large extent, we *all* suffer from a certain degree of fear. It is not only one of the three emotions, but the basis for them all. We are all driven by a fundamental fear of not getting what we want, or of getting what we *don't* want, which stirs up our other emotions. Desire usually involves a fear of being alone with ourselves and of not having enough, and anger comes from a fear of being threatened.

Fear also manifests in each of us as a deep ignorance that clouds and confuses our minds. Here, the term 'ignorance' does not mean a lack of education or information, but a level of delusion that makes us unaware of the true nature of things. It leaves us muddled by our deeply ingrained concepts and habits, and becomes the root cause of our pain and suffering.

## DESIRE

Desire includes all aspects of wanting, attachment, clinging, grasping and craving. We are constantly drawn to the things we see, hear, smell, taste or touch, as well as 'inner objects' of the mind, such as enjoyable thoughts and emotions. At first, desire usually feels pleasant, but it can make us, and those around us, suffer terribly.

The suffering comes from a frustrated lack of fulfilment and the fear of change. We never seem to have enough, and since everything is impermanent, nothing ever lasts, causing us to feel anxious. Our desire can take us into some dark places, where we get attached to *anything* – even, unwillingly, to things we don't like, such as unpleasant thoughts and emotions. We repeatedly get stuck, finding it almost impossible to break free.

The other side of desire is anger – the two go together. When we want something, we don't want something else. When we like something, we also dislike something. When we love, we have a similar capacity to hate – we can easily grow to hate whatever threatens that love. The constant push and pull between those two extremes of like and dislike can leave us feeling deeply unfulfilled.

Our strongest attachments usually occur in relationships. Of course, these can be healthy and positive, such as the deep love between a parent and child or other fulfilling connections, but when grasping and expectation take over, problems inevitably arise.

Perhaps we use the expression 'unconditional love' too freely, without recognising that it means to love *no matter what*. Very few people are truly able to embody that. Many relationships are built on the shaky ground of hope and fear, with an almost transactional quality: loving someone 'because', 'if' or 'when', rather than just for who they are. Maybe we want another person to 'complete' us, which is, of course, impossible. That type of 'conditional' love easily turns to anger, even hatred, when it is threatened.

The root of the problem is that because we don't recognise our own perfection, we feel incomplete and look elsewhere. We lack confidence and think we need to obtain happiness from the world around us. What we really seek is a sense of unity, which is often why people search for a partner. We fall in love without seeing how we project qualities onto the other person that we cannot find in ourselves. When the initial 'rush' wears off, we just as easily begin projecting faults onto them, and disappointment takes over. Sex is compelling because it allows for that feeling of unity and completeness, but only for a brief moment. Nothing seems to last or give us stable happiness. We are *always* trying to find our way home to that true inner perfection, searching everywhere but in the one place where it can actually be found – within ourselves.

Our desire for people and material objects can easily descend into needing, craving and wanting, which feels like drinking seawater to quench our thirst. The salt in the water simply makes us thirstier, and so we keep drinking more. We think of happiness as getting what we want, rather than understanding it as the freedom of *not* wanting, and so we remain constantly frustrated.

Our fundamental issue is that habits lead to more habits, which means our wanting creates more wanting, without bringing any lasting satisfaction. Because everything is impermanent, we cannot fully possess anything, as it is all subject to change, and so we feel perpetually frustrated. When we are caught up in desire, there is *always* that underlying feeling of not having enough. Regardless of what we have, we just feel more and more deprived.

## ANGER

Anger is the easiest emotion to identify, since it is so painful and destructive. Anger is the opposite of desire. It is not always felt as rage or hatred, as it includes all forms of dislike, such as irritation, frustration, discomfort – any type of aversion. It can be experienced at a very subtle level as the pushing away of any of the objects of our senses, including our own thoughts and emotions.

Anger generally leads to feelings of unhappiness and isolation. It brings almost immediate suffering to us and those around us. When driven by anger and aversion, we tend to see things in a narrow, extreme way and can even become fanatical. Sometimes we might think we *need* anger to get things done and to fight for necessary change. There is a better option, where action comes from a place of wisdom rather than from toxic habitual reactions. This will be explored in Chapter Seven: Compassion.

Anger leads to more anger. Because we have a tendency

to fight against whatever feels uncomfortable, there will always be something to dislike – we solve one problem, but our focus simply moves on to finding something else oppressive. This will not stop until we examine the emotion itself and begin to dismantle its habitual nature.

Anger usually feels either hot or cold: we become volcanic or like a block of ice. What we perhaps don't see is that when we are angry, we are projecting our feelings onto whomever or whatever has seemingly 'made' us angry, when in fact it is not the external challenge but our *reaction* that has created the anger. Several people will have different feelings about the same event, since there is never a situation independent of the perception of those who experience it.

It is all too easy to think, 'This person has made me angry.' On closer inspection, however, the statement lacks truth, as it implies I am a clean, blank canvas onto which that individual threw something nasty – they came along and did something that 'made' me angry. However, anger, as with all emotions, can only occur for me if I already possess the capacity to feel it, which means I also have the capacity to free myself. This is referred to in Buddhist philosophy as 'co-emergence' – as the problem arises, so too does the solution: within the anger lies the key to freedom from anger.

Why is anger so compelling and hard to let go of? As

with all our emotions, it is 'sticky' – our minds are addicted to holding on. Additionally, we don't like to lose ground, and so we hang on to our resentment. It would help us to realise that whenever we feel hurt by someone and grow angry and bitter, *they* have truly won the battle, as *we* are the one left suffering. Through forgiveness, we become invincible, and even if someone takes everything from us, they can never take our peace of mind.

## SUBTLE EMOTIONS

The Buddhist approach encourages us to look inside and explore the emotional undercurrents that drive us, making us constantly search for security. As we become more aware, we might see that whenever we reach for *anything*, we are reacting to a fleeting moment of anxiety, a subtle 'micro' fear. We are uncomfortable with the present moment and seek an escape. We fear the stillness and emptiness, we feel oppressed and want to move. We are addicted to *doing* rather than *being*, and so we keep ourselves busy. We have even invented complex technological devices so that we won't have to experience the present moment.

In general, when a painful emotion comes up, we tend to act on it because we are afraid simply to be with it and feel it. We might say or do regrettable things, all of which come from a place of wanting to get rid of our oppressive feelings, almost like someone trying to throw up after having eaten poison. As a result, we simply create more problems in our environment and in ourselves. The most courageous and compassionate thing we can ever do is to learn how to *be* with ourselves, thus breaking our habits and transcending our fears.

Those fears underpin so much in our lives. We are basically afraid of the present moment. We could go so far as to say we *hate* it, unless it is presenting us with some form of entertainment. This is why meditation at first seems so hard – to sit with nothing means to face that fear of stillness. It feels so difficult because we are not doing anything or getting anything.

People often hope that their meditation will provide a deeply relaxing escape from the harsh realities of the world, but quite the opposite is true – it is a journey of courage as we learn to face our thoughts and emotions. Through turning our attention inwards, we can begin to deal with the aspects of ourselves that our distractions have helped us to avoid looking at. We might feel nervous of how our practice will change us, as the notion of leaving behind our habits and addictions can be daunting. We have grown so comfortable with remaining trapped that the thought of *freedom* becomes frightening. We need to know that the happiness we seek can only be found through transforming our minds, which requires us to be brave and look within.

When exploring the nature of emotions, it is important to remember that they are never a problem if we learn how to relate to them properly. Fear, desire and anger are simply waves in the ocean of the mind. The suffering comes from our clinging, our habit of making those emotions feel too solid. We create complex stories about them and believe them to be real. Freedom comes from letting go of those stories, becoming aware and relaxing into what is being experienced, so that we can fully and unconditionally accept ourselves.

## MEDITATION EXERCISE:
## WORKING WITH THE EMOTIONS

Sit in a good posture and cultivate a motivation of loving-kindness and compassion, a reminder that you are meditating for the benefit of yourself and all others.

For this exercise, you are going to use visualisation, which means creating an image in your mind's eye.

Imagine that you are looking into a clear blue sky, or the night sky filled with stars. Visualise a small dot of light in the distance that starts to move closer to you, growing to become a sphere of gently swirling multicoloured lights. Try to feel that this ball of light symbolises the healing power of universal compassion.

The ball of light then turns into one colour, depending on which emotion you are working with.

**Fear: white light**
Then, imagine rays of white light begin to emanate from the sphere in front of you and fill your body. They connect with the places in you where you hold fear and anxiety, bringing a sense of comfort and healing.

**Desire: red light**
Next, ruby-red light rays emerge from the ball of light, filling your body. They contact your emotions of desire and grasping, easing the sufferings of the craving mind with their healing warmth.

**Anger: dark blue light**
Thirdly, dark blue rays emanate from the sphere of light, and they enter and spread throughout your body. They

reach into the places where you hold anger and resentment, or even just traces of mild irritation. The blue light brings a sense of peace and serenity, and your anger can begin to transform.

• • •

After you have practised each step, you may wish to return to one of them, to do some more work on whichever emotion is strongest for you.

To end your session, rest in a feeling that all your suffering has dissolved and that you now feel lighter and freer. Imagine that the light melts back into the sphere in front of you, which then returns to its original swirl of multi-coloured lights. Feel that it contains the purest possible love, compassion and wisdom, and it is then absorbed back into the horizon, becoming a tiny dot of light and vanishing into the sky.

Conclude with a few moments of relaxing in your body and mind, allowing your thoughts to come and go like clouds in the sky. Take a moment to dedicate your session to the happiness of all, and try to carry the feeling of the practice with you into your daily life.

# CHAPTER 5

# THE OBSERVER

'The opportunity to experience yourself
differently is always available.'

**MINGYUR RINPOCHE**

It took me a while to settle in at the monastery. I was
sure I had found my path, but the pull of my old life
would sometimes make me want to escape. I felt trapped,
even though nobody was forcing me to stay. I had always
been wary of organised religion, but it was reassuring to
me that Buddhism is more of a philosophy, encouraging
healthy debate and analysis. It certainly didn't seem like
I had joined a cult, but there was something making me
feel imprisoned. I began to realise it was my mind. I was
caught up inside my own head, in a tangle of painful
thoughts and emotions, but I could sense it was worth
persevering with the meditation, to go deeper and learn

to work with my suffering. I wanted to taste freedom, which I knew was not to be found in running away.

I immersed myself in Buddhist teachings on the mind, where I found rich material describing the power of observing one's thoughts and the nature of freedom. We all want to be free, but from *what*? I started to question whether this was something external or internal. I knew nobody could stop me from jumping over the monastery wall to run away, and then I would be 'free' – but *would* I? Would I have freed my mind?

The teachings I was studying explained that we are *not* our thoughts or feelings, and how connecting with our awareness allows us to observe. I found these ideas intriguing and empowering. I had felt tormented inside for a very long time, but here was a way to find the release I longed for, through changing the relationship between myself and my emotions.

Over time, I felt things begin to improve, and I was able to relax into being a monk. I felt happier and more positive. A few years into my monastic life, I was given an incredible opportunity: I became Akong Rinpoche's personal assistant. This meant spending most of my time around someone with extraordinary qualities, as well as experiencing his compassion in action through working by his side. I would assist him with his projects and accompany him on teaching tours. After a while, Rinpoche asked me to give my own talks, which I started doing when he was busy with his projects in Tibet.

Those talks took me into some interesting places, such as prisons, hospitals and addiction rehabilitation centres, as well as schools, universities and busy office environments. My aim was to bring meditation into highly stressful settings, where I felt it could make a real difference. I managed to find a way of presenting meditation in an accessible manner without using religious language, and people seemed open and receptive. Buddhist monks don't have a mission to convert others – in fact, it would be against our rules. Our intention is simply to offer whatever will help transform suffering and create genuine happiness.

I feel extremely lucky to work with such a variety of groups, ranging from children, prisoners and politicians to the inhabitants of remote villages in Africa. In turn, I also learn from them – the questions they ask, and how they approach meditation, help me to understand what people are looking for and what might help them. It has been fascinating to see what unifies these apparently disparate individuals: they all feel at the mercy of their own thoughts and feelings. They long to step back from the noise and set themselves free.

When I explain to them that meditation is not about numbing the mind or falling asleep, but connecting with awareness and becoming the observer, I notice how their eyes light up.

## DEEP DOWN, WE ARE ALL FREE

Meditation opened the door for me to *observe* my thoughts and emotions. I immediately found this approach compelling and wanted to explore it more deeply. It is a relatively advanced aspect of Buddhist philosophy, but it is helpful for us to know some of the theory as we continue on our journey. In terms of my own practice, I am still in the foothills of making these concepts a reality, but in this chapter I will share some technical details of what is meant by 'the observer', since it is such a fundamental area of knowledge that can help our meditation to progress.

Our first step is to acknowledge that in every moment of unhappiness, there is, at the same time, a part of ourselves free from the unhappiness. When we suffer, we usually *know* we are suffering. Does 'the knower' also suffer? We can feel our discomfort, but to *feel* it implies that the one who feels it, the part that knows we are suffering is *not* suffering. How else are we able to perceive and experience our discomfort? If we are aware that we are suffering and can observe it, our awareness itself is not suffering.

This insight is a major breakthrough, giving us the perspective that makes our journey to freedom finally seem possible. Meditation practice will deepen that understanding. The purpose of a technique such as focusing on the breath is to help us connect with our awareness, the part of the mind that watches the breath. We are learning to examine the relationship between our thinker and our thoughts, as well as our feeler and our feelings. By cultivating an ability to observe our minds, we can eventually discover that our awareness is the source of the freedom we have been seeking.

Awareness is like turning on the lights in a dark room. Even on our darkest days, it is our awareness that experiences the misery. The awareness itself cannot be dark, as only light can know darkness. No matter how bad things get, there is always a part of us which is free, and the more we meditate, the more we connect with that part. We connect with our own light.

In ancient Indian literature, one finds the example of a person in a dimly lit room who is terrified when they see a snake in the corner. As they draw closer, they realise it is simply a coiled rope. Their fear and panic dissolve, and they are able to relax. Nothing has changed other than their perception, and the story illustrates the power of awareness in showing us the true nature of things.

Our thoughts and feelings may just be ropes rather than snakes, but what if they are about pressing, challenging events, such as serious illness or bereavement? When I discuss this, for example, with people who are facing difficult medical situations, they often find that when they are able to see themselves as the observer of their sickness, they feel some relief and can move beyond being defined by their pain. They discover how to access a sense of freedom within their suffering.

## OUR NATURAL STATE

Even though it involves training, meditation is really a process of 'undoing' rather than 'doing'. When we sit down to meditate, we aren't actually *doing* anything, but simply relaxing into who we are. It is the doing nothing that brings results, rather than striving to become something else. This suggests that innate freedom and happiness are our natural state.

We often feel as if our pain and suffering are inevitable and inescapable. We might even assume we are 'hard-wired' to suffer. Suffering can certainly dominate our lives, but is it embedded within our true nature? Perhaps the very fact that we *dislike* it so much indicates a conflict with who we really are. If suffering were natural to us, would it feel so wrong and uncomfortable, so intrusive?

We can learn more about this by taking a closer look at our desire. One of our main habits is to chase after things, but when we get what we want, why is it that we feel fulfilled? It is because our desire has gone away. We are experiencing a sense of freedom, no longer troubled by the feeling of wanting. Interestingly, dopamine, the hormone associated with craving and anticipation, surges in our bodies during the 'chase', but then drops away just before we get what we want. The resulting happiness is simply an absence of wanting. This reveals how, through desire, we are simply trying to have no more desire. We constantly search for freedom, but keep reaching for things that keep us trapped. We look in the wrong places. Freedom can only be found within us, because that is where it was all along.

The Buddhist view is that suffering is *not* built into our true nature. We suffer because we don't realise we are actually happier than we thought. The happiness we always sought is already there, and we suffer because we have not yet harnessed our own power. We have assumed we need to look outside instead of tuning in to what is already there within us. Happiness, and suffering too, are simply states of mind.

We can only suffer because we also know its opposite. Suffering is a relative concept, possible because of its flip side – happiness and freedom from suffering. Suffering is only suffering because of happiness. Prison, for example, can only be prison because of the existence of the world outside its walls. Moreover, a prison is only possible because the prisoner locked within its cells also has the potential to be free. They would never be able to get out of there if the whole world were a prison – and if that were the case, the term 'prison' would not even exist.

We only suffer because, deep down, we are truly free. We remain imprisoned for now, because we don't fully know ourselves and haven't recognised our inner potential. We suffer because we don't realise we are already perfect, and thus we seek perfection in the world around us. We long to go beyond our suffering and limitations, which implies that freedom is innate to us.

Our true potential, our 'deeper' mind, has none of the constraints of feeling happy or sad and the ups and downs of our lives. It is described in traditional meditation texts as beyond concept, ineffable, intangible, completely open, like space or the sky, and possessing the qualities of profound happiness, compassion and wisdom. Meditation connects us with that essence, helping us to transform our suffering and achieve liberation.

## NOTHING IS REAL

According to Buddhist philosophy, our problems ultimately come from our habit of taking everything to be real – material objects, people, situations and, crucially, even our thoughts and emotions. In believing these to be solid and absolute, we react to them with attachment and aversion, which causes pain and a feeling that there is no hope of any change. It is due to their insubstantiality, however, that things *can* change. Freedom is only possible because our suffering has no ultimate or solid reality that needs to be broken down or removed.

Buddhism points out that reality does not truly exist in the way it appears, a view now shared in the world of cutting-edge quantum physics. If we take a more precise look at everything we experience, we cannot find anything but our own mental creations – and even those lack any real substance.

If we examine something even as tangible as a table, for example, and investigate its true nature, we might discover it is not as real as we thought. If we take the table apart and remove its legs, is it still a table? Breaking down those pieces even further, we arrive at a pile of wood shavings, and eventually particles. Can we find the smallest component? Is there a 'part-less particle', the tiniest foundation of all matter? Surely if it is a particle, it has parts and can be further divided into yet smaller particles. When we look at a table, it is just the coming together of many things, each lacking any single inherent reality. It even depends upon the perception of the person experiencing and naming the table, and so it relies on multiple factors for its existence.

Scientists built the 'atom smasher' in Switzerland to find the smallest particle. The Large Hadron Collider at CERN near Geneva was designed to seek out what is sometimes referred to as 'the God Particle'. The working hypothesis is that this tiniest part of an atom comes together with others like it, as the building blocks for our reality. Buddhists, however, would argue that if you can find it, then it still has constituent parts and is further divisible, so there is no finite base which makes up our universe. Buddhists would say that regardless of how many atoms you try to smash, you will never find the smallest component, even at the subatomic level. There is truly nothing to hold on to.

Our rigid concepts of reality fall apart under investigation, for they are merely relative – rather than ultimate – facts. Up, down, left and right, can only exist in relation to one another – there is no true up or down. The present moment is simply what is designated as a period between the past and the future, but as soon as we try to pin it down, it has already become the past. There *is* no present moment. We cling to our fixed ideas, but perhaps everything is more of an illusion than we had previously assumed.

## DO *WE* EXIST?

Are we our bodies, or are we our thoughts and emotions? Who *are* we? The Buddhist approach uses a process of investigation and logic to track down who we think we are, with the aim of breaking down our inflexible beliefs about reality.

Does this 'self' of ours really exist? We could try to find its location. Am I my body, or am I *in* my body? What happens if I lose a limb – does my 'self' diminish by a corresponding amount? If my body were cut into tiny pieces and then spread across a field, I would, of course, be dead, but where is that thing I have been calling 'me'? When the parts are separated, is the self now in many places? Furthermore, is my mind *in* my body, *or* is my body in my mind? Surely it is my mind that experiences my body? Can we truly find the 'I' within this psycho-physical collection of elements that we call the 'self'?

What of the mind, then? Are we our thoughts? We tend to define ourselves through how we think and feel, but we could investigate further and ask ourselves if those thoughts and emotions are truly real. Where do they come from and where do they go to? We often use the phrase, 'a thought has popped into my head' – but from where?

We seem to think of thoughts and feelings as *separate* from us, as if they are objects 'within' our minds, 'coming in' from somewhere else, and consequently, when they disturb us, we want to get rid of them. The Buddhist view is that they are inseparable from our minds, just like waves in the ocean. Our tension comes from thinking of thoughts and emotions as being distinct from the mind itself, and we remain convinced that we must either fight and push back against them or *do* something about them. We don't know whether to go with them, to try to change them or to send them away. Each option just seems to make things worse.

In our confusion, we attribute a sense of solidity and concrete reality to the mind and whatever it thinks and feels, surrendering and taking it all as real, even though it constantly changes and none of it has any tangible substance. We easily believe the negative stories we tell ourselves and become afraid of those stories, leading to more tension and misery.

If our thoughts and emotions were real, how would there be enough space inside us for them all? Where are they? To be real, they must have defining characteristics such as location, size or shape, and the mind itself would need to be located and have a centre and edges. Perhaps they are more like a rainbow, 'there but not there', or a mirage, and we don't need to *believe* in them so much, fearfully being led by them, fighting an endless losing battle.

## THE OBSERVER

Continuing this line of enquiry, who is it that does all this thinking? Who is it that watches the thoughts when we meditate? Who is the 'observer'? I once asked a neuro-scientist friend about this, and he laughed and said, 'Oh, we haven't found that bit yet.' In Buddhism, the *'not finding'* is the key to raising questions that help us transcend our limiting concepts and beliefs.

Having established that we are not our thoughts, emotions or suffering, are we, then, the 'observer'? Our habit of seeking solid ground may tempt us to fix upon an idea of a 'super-mind'. We would like jubilantly to declare that who we *really* are is the observer of our thoughts, but this simply means we have not gone far enough in our analysis of the mind.

We are simply trying to replace the small self with a bigger self, and thus the observer becomes our 'new' self. We are still missing the point, however, falling into what is described in Buddhist texts as the reification or 'thingification' of awareness or the observer. We need to understand that even the observer has no solid, intrinsic reality.

If we were to examine the observer – awareness, the part of us that perceives our thoughts – we would now have an observer looking at the observer. There could even be *another* observer looking at the observer of the observer. Where does it end? If we cannot find the source, the 'furthest-back' observer, who are we?

The renowned meditation master Chögyam Trungpa said, 'The bad news is you're falling through the air, nothing to hang on to, no parachute. The good news is, there's no ground.' The aim of all these explorations is to reduce our habit of clinging to phenomena – even ourselves – as being real, since it is the solidification that makes us suffer, and then to become comfortable with the *not* finding, the *not* knowing.

These are some of the most profound aspects of Buddhist philosophy, and they are hard to grasp, but it is helpful to remain open to the idea that all is not as it seems. Advanced practitioners are able to use these investigations within their meditation practice and can transcend the level of conceptual thinking, but the rest of us are still at the stage of an intellectual, academic appreciation of these notions – and I include myself here. This is because we are using concepts in trying to go beyond concept.

This is not a problem. We are still at the start of our journey, and it is enough to begin with a simple acknowledgement that we have a habit of over-solidifying our experiences. Over time, this will be dismantled by our meditation practice, eventually leading us to discover the true meaning of freedom.

## MEDITATION EXERCISE: THE SKY

This practice is inspired by the concepts explored in this chapter. It helps you to connect with your awareness, your ability to observe your mind. It also begins to dissolve the habit of grasping at thoughts and emotions as being solid or real.

This time, you are going to look at the actual sky, rather than just imagining it. Sit where you can see the sky, either outdoors or by a window.

Begin your session by establishing compassion, setting the intention that you are meditating for the benefit of others as well as yourself.

As you look into the sky, feel that your mind and the sky are mixing together, becoming one.

Try to feel that your mind is just like the sky, vast and without centre, edges or limitations. Your thoughts and emotions are like clouds, passing through the sky.

Distractions will take your mind elsewhere, but just keep bringing your attention back to the sky. Try to feel how those distractions have a transparent nature, as though you can look through them into the spacious backdrop behind them. Everything takes place within that great expanse, completely inseparable from it.

You are observing the sky with your eyes and observing your mind with itself.

When you are ready to end the session, spend a few moments focusing on your body and its contact with the chair or the ground.

The last step is another moment of compassion, where you again remember that you are meditating to develop the wisdom and compassion needed to bring real benefit to others as well as yourself.

# CHAPTER 6
# ACCEPTANCE

**'What you resist persists.'**
**CARL JUNG**

Twelve years after joining the monastery, I decided to enter a strict four-year-long meditation retreat on a remote Scottish island. I wanted to deepen my practice through highly intensive training. The retreat would involve being completely cut off from the outside world, without news, phones or internet, and following a strict programme of around 16 hours of meditation every day. We would be a group of 21 monks, mainly meditating alone in our rooms in the small complex of buildings of a converted farmhouse. We could get fresh air by walking around the courtyard but never beyond the boundary walls. Food was to be brought in each day by a caretaker living on the outside of the retreat compound.

I travelled to the island in the summer of 2005, nervous but keen to get started. After saying goodbye to friends and family who had come to see us off, the retreat began with a special ceremony to 'seal' the buildings. I think we all felt somewhat daunted as we sat in our dimly lit dining room and it dawned on us that this would be our entire world for the next four years. Rinpoche gave a short talk, which was simple and direct. I can remember him saying, 'You are here to learn how to die.' His words were startling and hard-hitting, but I trusted him and knew we were being given the chance to taste a deeper level of practice and to cultivate our inner strength. It was a stark reminder that when death approaches, the only thing that matters is our state of mind. The same is true in all other times of crisis.

Our days began at 3.45am and ended at 11pm, with a rigorous schedule of meditation sessions, each lasting two or three hours. We were learning ancient practices, handed down over the centuries through Tibetan lineages, but the methods always felt fresh and timeless. Life in retreat was a curious mixture of the mystical and the mundane, with profound meditations punctuated by set mealtimes, bells to announce session times and a cleaning rota. Our group ranged in age from 30 to 70 and came from several countries. Our diet consisted of a light breakfast, with lunch as the main meal and no food in the evenings. We were encouraged not to lie down at night but to sleep upright, in order to stay more connected to the meditation. Teachers would regularly visit the retreat to provide guidance and instruction, and Rinpoche came to see us once a year.

It was a supportive environment, but I soon began to struggle, hitting difficulties after only a couple of weeks. The problems I had experienced during previous retreats came flooding back, but this time much worse. Distressing emotions and a deep sense of trauma grew incredibly vivid, and I could feel them spreading through my body like a dark cloud. I knew not to expect bliss and rainbows from my meditation, but this was a whole new level of suffering, and I was shocked. I now see it was a crucial part of being in retreat – to sit with my own mind – but at the time, it was horrible and extremely challenging.

In the second year, we took vows of silence for five months, which made the experience feel even more solitary. All the noise in my head intensified and I felt backed into a corner with my own thoughts. I had to encounter parts of myself I had been hiding from, such as painful memories of abuse when I was younger. My state of mind grew bleak and oppressive, and on many days I felt as if I was falling through space into an abyss. There were times when I could not meditate at all, but would just lie on the floor in a state of horror.

Soon after the silent period ended, I felt I had reached the end of my capacity to handle any more pain. The panic attacks of my youth had returned with full force, along with episodes of severe depression, and I was not coping. This was not simply a case of being unhappy – in my experience, depression is a serious devastation of the psyche, which becomes dangerously dark, at times devoid of any feeling at all, as if one's brain has gone completely 'offline'.

I wanted to die, but felt even that would not be enough. I longed for complete annihilation, and the idea of mere death seemed puny and inadequate. I wanted somehow to be deleted from the entire universe – my tormented mind needed something *more* than death. I was rapidly heading downhill and my suffering was getting out of control.

I also felt a great deal of shame – I was one of the senior monks in the retreat, but was now spectacularly falling apart in front of everyone. I felt terribly ashamed of my depression. Monks are supposed to be serene and 'sorted', not depressed and wanting to kill themselves.

The retreat leaders and my fellow monks tried their best to support me, but I was too far gone to be reached and wasn't able to hear anything they were telling me.

One morning I just lost it, and in a frenzy, I ran to the boundary of the retreat compound and jumped over the fence. I landed on the other side in brambles and mud, experiencing a full-blown panic attack. My heart was beating extremely fast, I was bathed in sweat and felt as if my head would burst. I then found myself running down the road through heavy rain. I didn't get very far – something inside told me to stop and turn around.

I came back to the edge of the retreat enclosure to find the caretaker making anxious phone calls to the monastery. This was a major event, and naturally, my fellow monks would have felt rattled by what had happened. In such a serious retreat, it is unthinkable to jump over the fence and break the boundary. I knew I was in trouble.

Quite soon, however, my mind became surprisingly clear and stable. Maybe I was in shock, but I felt a sudden and powerful sense of purpose. Highly focused, I was convinced with every fibre of my being of what I really wanted, which was to stay and continue with the retreat. I begged to be given another chance and sought permission to spend a week living just outside the boundary, where I wanted to find a way to prove myself.

I was determined, and Lama Yeshe, the abbot of the monastery, said he was willing to test me. On the edge of a muddy field, away from the retreat, there was a tiny old caravan without electricity or running water. I asked if I could stay there for a week, to meditate and think deeply about what had happened.

Over the several days spent in that caravan, listening to the wild wind and rain of the bleak island weather, my mind began to transform at a rapid pace. Pennies were dropping in quick succession, and I could feel my tight grip on the depression and fear loosening, letting them fall away. I sensed that something within me had been exposed – to myself – and the game was now up. I had been deluding myself into thinking I *was* my misery and that it somehow defined me. I could also see how I had been using it to get sympathy from others, since I had no idea of how to be kind to myself.

I firmly wanted to continue with the retreat. Lama Yeshe gave me permission to go back in, but only if I made a non-negotiable commitment to properly engage with the programme. I was happy to do this. I knew I had to work *with* my pain or it would destroy me, and that I needed to surrender to the meditation practices. Most importantly, I had to discover the right attitude for handling my turbulent emotions.

I returned to my retreat room and rejoined the schedule. The other monks were understandably a little wary – I had broken a holy space, a sealed retreat – and to this day, I remain immensely grateful that they accepted me back in. I was now ready to dive fully into the practices, and everything began to change. Of course, there were still challenges – retreat is never smooth or easy, and difficult feelings would still come up – but the 'breakthrough' came from discovering I could sit with my suffering without pushing it away, instead simply *allowing* it and offering it love and compassion. I experimented with relaxing *into* my pain, dropping resistance and welcoming it.

My experience of the retreat was now very different. Until that point, I had found everything intolerable, with a recurring mental image of myself trapped within an iron ball with sharp spikes on the inside. With every move I made, I would feel those spikes dig into me as the ball rolled about. Now, as I began to struggle less, I often felt surprisingly comfortable, as if wrapped in a warm duvet, and my meditation practice took on a remarkably different flavour.

A few months later, Akong Rinpoche came for his annual visit. With some trepidation, I went to his room and told him what had happened – that I had broken all the rules and done such a shocking thing. Some of the other retreatants were convinced I would be given a severe telling-off, or even be asked to leave. However, to my relief, Rinpoche simply stroked the top of my head, and said, 'Well done,' in the softest, kindest voice I had ever heard. I felt he was the one person who understood what had really happened to me.

I instinctively knew, unconventional though it was, that my running away and coming back was the key which had unlocked a strength within me, and Rinpoche seemed to know that too.

For the remainder of the four years my meditation felt like medicine, and I wanted more of it. For the first time in my life, I was able to enjoy my own company. The rigours of the daily schedule were still a challenge, but one I welcomed and saw as helpful. Today, having lived through that experience, I find it impossible to get depressed. It feels as though a powerful and destructive habit has died.

What I learned in that retreat was that when I can 'merge' with my pain and 'become one' with it, it cannot really hurt me. There is less of a feeling that something *over there* is bothering someone *over here*. Instead, through acceptance, a feeling of 'oneness' emerges. This allows the suffering to melt, and even to turn into sensations of deep inner joy as resistance falls away. Of course, I still go through difficult times, but I now know what to do. It is quite surprising, and if you too can move closer to your pain, you might find you can handle it in ways you never dreamed possible.

## ACCEPTANCE

I always found the word 'acceptance' heavy and oppressive, as if we are being told to 'put up with' our suffering, to 'grin and bear it'. It felt depressing and harsh. It was a revelation to discover that acceptance actually means to embrace the present moment unconditionally, even when that moment is unpleasant. This conveys a sense of warmth, even of love, rather than miserably carrying a burden with grim resignation. When seen in that light, acceptance is much closer to kindness and compassion. It is a radical type of happiness that fills us with great courage.

If you want to find a way out of suffering, the solution is never to run away, but to accept your feelings and move closer to the discomfort. You can try all kinds of things to escape. You can jump over the wall of your 'retreat' and run screaming down the road, but your problems will simply accompany you like a shadow. Only when you find a way to go back *in* and face the pain, can real change occur.

You might think that to focus on your pain will increase it, but the opposite is true – when resistance is gone, your suffering can no longer hurt you. When you shy away from suffering you amplify it, by feeding the habit of pushing away discomfort. As Jung says, 'What you resist persists.'

There is an interesting and relevant expression, 'grasping the nettle', which means to tackle an issue boldly and with strength. Nettles are plants that sting and cause pain if you brush past them or touch them lightly, but not if you grab them firmly. When you take hold of a nettle in a strong and deliberate manner, you are much less likely to get stung.

We can learn to deal with our suffering in a similar way, by taking a firm hold of it. To slide past it or approach it timidly just gives the suffering more power, causing it to become stronger and more painful. If, however, we take a good look at our unhappiness and use it as meditation, we are grasping the nettle and will not get stung. What initially seems threatening can even become nourishing. Nettles, when used in the right way, make a healthy and delicious soup or tea.

## PAIN CAN HELP US GROW

Nothing is ever wasted. In the work of agriculture and gardening, compost is made from rotten vegetables. What some people might discard, others use to make their fields and gardens flourish. Similarly, if we can view our dark and difficult experiences more creatively, they will begin to enhance our practice and help us become free. The 'rotten' aspects of our lives, and of ourselves – those parts of us we usually want to reject – are the very things that can wake us up, shaking us out of our complacency and making us stronger. Just as the beautiful lotus flower grows in murky water, our perfection emerges from the 'mess' of our lives.

There is nothing wrong with feeling bad. Our pain, mental or physical, is a chance to discover something truthful about ourselves. When we are broken, when the hard times have overwhelmed us, the rigid shell of our ego has been somewhat dismantled and we are left feeling raw. It is a profoundly honest moment. As the ego's habits fall away, we experience the collapse of a game that we have been unconsciously playing, of seeking happiness outside ourselves and blaming the world for our problems. This time, we didn't get our way and the game is up, at least for now. We can either fall back into our habits and distractions and start to chase things again, or we can learn, through meditation, to stay with the painful moment and embrace the sadness. This transforms our practice into a meaningful and effective *path* rather than just a search for a quick fix.

What is a path? It only exists as the way through life's obstructions, without which it would not be needed. We only create a path in a forest, for example, to help people find their way through the thick trees. Meditation practice is a journey, rather than a random single experience, and the purpose of the path is to take us through our obstacles. Working on those obstacles *is* the path.

Hard times, then, are integral features of that path, and they can be very good for us. Most importantly, they encourage an awakening of our innate sense of compassion as we realise we aren't alone in our suffering but are sharing in something deeply human. Through embracing the suffering, we can generate a sense of unconditional love and compassion towards ourselves, which is the foundation for compassion for others, as we begin to understand the common experience of pain that is the human condition.

## DROPPING RESISTANCE

The thinking behind the practice of acceptance is both radical and transformative. The more we realise that hard times are an opportunity, the more we can drop our resistance. This means letting go of our unwillingness to suffer. Initially, that could sound dangerous, as though we might just walk out in front of moving traffic, but the idea isn't to seek out suffering. Instead, when it comes into our lives, we can liberate ourselves by cultivating a mentality of non-resistance.

Through deciding that hard times are helpful for our development, we are giving up our *unwillingness* to suffer, and in doing so, our pain is left with no more ground or power. We will no longer allow ourselves to be bullied by it. We are training in abandoning the thought 'I don't want to suffer' – since that is what makes us suffer in the first place. 'I don't want to suffer' is a habit which simply creates more 'I don't want to suffer', and so there will always be problems.

By giving up that habitual way of thinking, we will *not* suffer. Ironically, then, through deciding that we don't mind it, or even quite like it, we will *stop* suffering, because unhappiness is a mental attitude. Of course, we may have tangible pain in our body, even a broken leg, or we might be facing a terrible disaster. It goes without saying that we should seek help and medical treatment when necessary, but how we react to those situations, our state of mind from moment to moment, is what really counts. The *suffering* comes from our deeply ingrained belief that we must push away all discomfort. That mindset is vigorously promoted in today's culture, placing us under great pressure to be happy, always to have a good time, to keep busy and achieve things, and, most importantly, *never* to suffer.

## BREAKING THE CODE

Our suffering is the key to our freedom, because it is the very thing that enables us to remove the habit of resistance. Since the 'I don't want to suffer' is what needs to be dismantled, it is helpful that it comes up whenever we hit difficulties. The suffering has allowed us to see it, drawing it out of its hiding place.

This allows us to break a code, to find the secret message hidden within every challenging situation: through suffering, we meet our fear of suffering, and by transforming that, we can find true freedom. The problem *is* the solution – *because* of it, we can do the work of melting down our resistance. The pain itself has freed us, making us fearless.

We shouldn't expect overnight results, but these methods set us on a path that will consistently chip away at *how* we suffer. There is, however, a definitive 'code-breaking' moment, as when we have understood the mechanics, something has been exposed and we have found the key. From that moment on, we cannot continue in ignorance. We will still struggle, but with the knowledge that every difficult experience is the portal to our freedom.

## MEDITATING ON SUFFERING

The practice of acceptance is a very deep form of meditation. We are familiar with focusing on our breath as a support, but *anything* can be used in this way, even suffering itself. We can meditate 'on' our discomfort, whether that be emotional or physical, and in doing so, we are transforming how we feel about it and how that affects us.

When we assign something as our meditation support, our relationship with it changes. We are drawn back to it after getting lost in distraction. When our minds wander, we gently come back to the support, making that the place where we want to be. We feel *attracted* to it. By using discomfort in this way, it becomes a help rather than a hindrance, something to bring us into the present moment. We will suffer less, as our suffering has been made into the object of our meditation.

A key component in meditation practice is the letting go of judgements – our ideas of things being good or bad, pleasant or unpleasant. Instead, we can just *be* with our experiences without exaggerating them or pushing them away. When welcomed, everything becomes our friend. If we apply this attitude to difficult situations, we are building habits of acceptance and resilience that can completely transform our lives.

## MERGING

The principal method for acceptance is to meditate *on*, or even *within*, our suffering. We can only do this if we let go of the narrative, the 'storyline', the 'He said this, she did that', the 'Why did this happen?' or 'Why me?' Once we learn to stop listening to those thoughts, we enter a space where we can move closer to the pain and discomfort.

Through dropping the storyline, it is easier to become one with our suffering. This means focusing on it and completely relaxing into it. What lies beneath it is an emotion, and the practice is to place our attention on how that emotion feels in our bodies. It usually has a physical resonance, such as a tightness or heaviness in the chest, belly or another area. Once we have located it, we can move closer.

There is no reason for concern – suffering cannot hurt us if we *become* it. The practice skilfully dismantles the sense of 'I' am being hurt by 'it', with something 'over there' harming someone 'over here'. Instead, there is simply a feeling of oneness. I like to call this practice 'merging'. It takes away the 'sting' from our pain – and eventually, how we experience it will start to change in ways we never could have imagined.

It is not easy to jump straight into the practice of merging. We need, as preparation, some experience of the basic meditation techniques, such as focusing on the breathing. Through using our breath as a support, we become less addicted to our thoughts and feelings, and thus less likely to fly off into those mental storylines. More significantly, it is essential that we first learn *how* to observe, how to step back, as only then can we truly merge – we stepped back so that we can now move towards, as we have discovered the part of our minds that can do the merging.

## MEDITATION EXERCISE: MERGING

Begin your session by sitting in a good posture and then plant the seed of compassion by reminding yourself that you are meditating for your own benefit and the benefit of others.

Next, spend a few minutes meditating on your breathing. Remember to breathe naturally, without altering anything.

The main practice is to focus your attention on the place in your body where you feel some discomfort, the physical expression of your emotional state. As you become aware of that sensation, your mind will keep slipping away into distractions, such as the storylines – the internal monologue *about* your suffering. When you realise you have lost focus, simply come back to the feeling in your body.

Bring your mind and the feeling closer together. Try not to get caught up in judgements, labels of 'good' or 'bad'. Move closer, and let your mind become one with your suffering. You and your uncomfortable feelings are now inseparable, with a sense of unity, of oneness.

You are not trying to get rid of anything, but simply being with the discomfort. You are befriending your emotions, willingly entering into an unconditional relationship with your own distress and pain.

When you are ready to end the session, spend a few moments just relaxing, feeling your body's contact with the chair or the ground beneath you. Conclude the practice with another moment of compassion, reminding yourself that you are meditating for the benefit of all.

• • •

Merging is a daily practice, rather than a 'one-off' solution, so it needs to be done again and again, whenever suffering arises in your life.

It is important not to allow the process to become cold and clinical, telling yourself, 'I *must* now meditate on my suffering,' with the grim determination of someone going into battle. Instead, merging is an experience of genuine loving-kindness and compassion. Think about how you would behave towards a scared child, a friend in crisis or a frightened animal. You would sit calmly with them and be there for them, without any judgement or blame.

The practice of merging is similar to falling in love, where the boundaries between yourself and another person have dissolved. Love can sometimes feel as if you are both made of water, and a similar sensation arises when you meditate on merging with your pain. As you move closer, the suffering can no longer hurt you, as you are unified with it. You have mixed together and become one.

# CHAPTER 7
# COMPASSION

**'My religion is kindness.'**
**THE DALAI LAMA**

The kindest person I have ever known was my teacher, Akong Rinpoche. He had an incredibly deep understanding of human suffering, and was completely devoted to helping others. I never saw him being negative or selfish, and those who met him came away feeling uplifted, loved and accepted. He was able to help people get to the roots of their problems and find solutions. In his teachings and advice, he would constantly encourage us to develop our compassion.

In his youth, Rinpoche went through extremely hard times. When China invaded Tibet in 1959, he was forced out of his homeland into exile. With a group of 300 people, he and his closest friends left their monastery by stealth and embarked on a perilous journey, crossing treacherous Himalayan mountain passes on foot, travelling mainly by night to avoid being captured. Their escape to the safety of India took almost a year. Of the 300, only 13 survived.

The food they had taken with them ran out after a month, and they were unable to make a fire to cook anything, in case the smoke attracted the attention of the Chinese army. There were no vegetables to be found in the snowy mountains, and they didn't want to kill any animals due to their Buddhist beliefs. They ended up resorting to eating their own shoes and belts, trying to obtain whatever nourishment they could. Most of the group died from starvation or were shot or captured.

Eventually, they had nothing left to eat or drink and were huddled in a cave in the mountains, waiting for death. Rinpoche later told me that as he lay on the rocky ground with his surroundings swimming in front of his eyes due to hunger, he made a firm promise to himself: should he survive, he would devote his entire life to feeding the hungry, as he could now feel their pain and understand their suffering. Fortunately, he and his friends were rescued by some hunters who stumbled upon their cave and guided them to food and safety.

The 13 survivors, exhausted and emaciated, reached India, where they were placed in refugee camps with others who had also fled their home country. As the Tibetans began to organise themselves into communities, Rinpoche helped to run a little school in the hills of North India. After a couple of years, he and a few others were sent to the UK, where they initially settled in Oxford. Rinpoche applied to work at the local hospital. He had received an advanced training in Tibetan medicine, but because his qualifications were not recognised in the West, the hospital employed him as a porter and cleaner.

These were challenging years for Rinpoche. He had lost his homeland, family and friends. He had been brought up as the highly respected leader of a monastery in Tibet, but was now a refugee in completely new surroundings. He struggled with deep feelings of loss, but found that his meditation and training in acceptance helped him make the best of a very difficult situation.

It was not long before people began to hear about him and his Tibetan colleagues, as word travelled that they were eminent Buddhist teachers. At that time, there was a growing interest in Eastern philosophy and particularly Tibetan Buddhism. In 1967, Rinpoche and his friends founded Samye Ling Monastery in Scotland, which is where his skills and care for others began to shine. As the monastery developed, Rinpoche offered guidance to the many people who came to him seeking teachings on meditation, and he became a key figure in establishing Buddhism in the UK.

After some years, his work expanded to other countries, enabling him to fulfil his wish of helping the poor and destitute. He set up soup kitchens and other charitable projects in some of the world's most deprived areas. He was now able to make regular visits to his homeland of Tibet, where he and his organisation provided homes, food and education for more than 10,000 people every year.

Rinpoche was a powerful example of a human being's capacity for profound compassion and how we can all contribute to making our world a happier and kinder place. The fundamental principle of his message was that these qualities are natural to who we are, which we simply need to uncover.

## NATURAL COMPASSION

*Are* we made of love and compassion? The 17th-century philosopher Thomas Hobbes, author of *Leviathan*, would probably disagree, as he famously (and rather depressingly) stated that without a 'social contract' to keep us in check, life on this planet would simply be 'nasty, brutish and short'. His detractors have amusingly suggested he was really just describing himself, but he has certainly provided us with an interesting debate around what it means to be human.

Is life just a race for the survival of the fittest, the daily struggle of maintaining our existence, or do we have a deeper purpose? We humans crave connection and community, and are most at ease when we encounter kindness. We like to communicate and help each other out. In general, it feels good to be kind. In that case, perhaps we are here for one another?

Our internal chemistry is at its healthiest whenever we are experiencing compassion: our bodies fill with oxytocin, the 'bonding' hormone, which puts us in a state of love and happiness. This first occurs when we are born and then placed on our mother's chest, allowing us to feel calm and protected. Throughout our lives, we are reintroduced to oxytocin with every experience of kindness.

Genuine happiness is only possible when we *honour* our link with others, rather than living from a place of separation and conflict, which only generates the stress hormones cortisol and adrenaline. These deplete our energy levels, leaving us unhappy and exhausted. They are simply not good for us. Whenever there is an awareness of connection, we are at our happiest and feel the most alive.

Of course, human actions can often descend into the 'nasty and brutish', but always as behaviour rather than our true nature. The negativity feels like an aberration, not something intrinsic to who we are. We can only survive through compassion, and the Buddhist perspective would view the Hobbesian model of a competitive and vicious society as a philosophical construct rather than a reflection of the real world.

## A CURE FOR SUFFERING

Buddhism encourages a bringing together of the wisdom of the mind with the heart's capacity for love and kindness. Blaise Pascal, a significantly more cheerful 17th-century philosopher, spoke of the intelligence of the heart, and how the constant division between our heads and our hearts brings suffering into our lives. Buddhists would agree that a greater integration of wisdom and compassion strengthens our ability to connect with others, allowing happiness to become a universal goal rather than a fruitless chase only focused on the self.

We suffer because we run after pleasure and resist

discomfort, causing us to feel dissatisfied and afraid of pain. We keep ourselves trapped in that cycle, which means that ultimately, the source of our suffering is none other than ourselves. Compassion is the best remedy, and far from leading us into self-denial or avoidance, it makes us less preoccupied with our own problems, as we discover a wider perspective. When we remove our own suffering from under the microscope, we will find the way to greater happiness for ourselves and others.

As long as we remain enslaved by our egos, nobody wins – we become insensitive to the people around us, and our own needs are never fulfilled. Compassion, on the other hand, creates a 'win–win' scenario: others benefit, and we too achieve sustainable happiness and freedom. The Dalai Lama famously said that we all tend to be selfish, but in a 'stupid' way, since we only look out for ourselves, which never leads to lasting satisfaction. He advised that we instead become selfish in a 'wise' way, by shifting our focus to include everyone else, which will strengthen our own happiness. That is the win–win situation.

Compassion is based on our innate intelligence. We understand that just as we want to be happy, others too have a natural desire for happiness and freedom. Everyone has the right to fulfil those fundamental wishes, and as we live in an interconnected world where everything depends on something else for its existence, we are one family. No matter how different we might appear, our goals are similar, and we are all essentially walking the same path. Through recognising that shared experience, we can feel closer, generating a more expansive and universal sense of love and compassion. We discover that when we pull together to work for the greater good of all, we can achieve real happiness. We learn how to dissolve the boundaries between self and other.

When Akong Rinpoche was guiding the volunteers at one of his soup kitchens in Nepal, he advised them that instead of walking down the rows of seated homeless people and ladling out the soup into their bowls, they could try kneeling in front of each recipient and respectfully making an offering of the food. He said it is only through those who need our help that we can develop our compassion, so perhaps we should show them the same reverence as if meeting the Buddha. Perhaps it is they who are helping us.

Compassion is a position of deep respect, where we understand the nature of suffering, connect with the pain of others and feel grateful for the opportunity to be of assistance. Crucially, it is an acknowledgement of not just their obvious, surface pain, but also what is 'hidden' – the latent, often subtle, discomfort that people carry within themselves.

Another time at the soup kitchen, the volunteers told

Rinpoche that sometimes people would come for food who were clearly not at all poor, and they didn't know whether or not to serve them. Rinpoche said that even if someone pulls up in a limousine, they should be given soup and kindness, as nobody knows what suffering that person might secretly be going through.

We tend not to look very deeply, and if someone appears to be alright, we assume they are not suffering. Does someone need to fall apart in front of us before we feel they deserve our compassion? The Buddhist view is that we *all* carry layers of pain and distress which are often buried and unseen. Genuine compassion is where we connect with the whole picture of a person rather than just what they show to the world.

It can be argued that today, the work of inner transformation and a recognition of our interconnectedness are no longer luxuries but necessities. Globally, we have arrived at a state of emergency, where we must either learn to be more tolerant and compassionate or risk annihilation. As we progress in our meditation and become more sensitive to the complexity of suffering, we will increasingly feel the urge to do something to be of help. It is that call to action which underpins true compassion, reinforced by consistent training of the mind.

## THE EMPATHY QUESTION

Buddhism sees compassion as more than just an emotional reaction. The difference between feeling sorry for someone and doing something to help them is what separates empathy from compassion. Empathy means we somehow join with their suffering, as it comes from a place of feelings and reactions.

Empathy is like being in a boat, a person falls overboard and we jump into the water to save them but don't know how to swim. As a result, we both drown together. Compassion is where we reach out and pull them back onto the boat. Compassion is dynamic and purposeful, bringing tangible results.

According to neurological research, empathy activates the brain's 'mirror neurons': when we encounter others in pain, those neurons are triggered in us, and we feel their suffering too. We wince and recoil when seeing someone break their arm, even if only in a film. We almost experience their pain. Empathy has its merits – at least we are thinking of others – but ultimately, it is not particularly useful. If someone is suffering and I am crying about it, they could easily say, 'Thank you for your tears, but they don't actually help me.'

Empathy is by no means bad for us, but on its own, it

lacks power and can become draining. It often leads to 'empathic distress' with intense feelings of overwhelm. As we have seen, compassion goes further than our emotions. It is a wise and potent state of being that leads to positive, helpful action. Instead of sinking into misery when we meet suffering, if we develop our compassion we are learning how to get out there and do something about it.

## COMPASSION AS A PROJECT

When we first encounter Buddhism, it can be confusing that its teachings talk so much about compassion, and yet its practitioners seem to spend their time sitting in a room staring into space. Some even go into solitary meditation retreats for many years. One might wonder how they think they are helping anyone.

What does it mean to help others? We can alleviate their 'symptoms' by offering kindness and immediate aid, which is of course important and useful. A deeper approach is also to show them how *not* to suffer. This requires us to unearth the hidden reasons *behind* the suffering, which we must first discover in ourselves. If we can liberate our own minds from what *really* makes us suffer – our habits of resistance and reactivity – we will then possess the wisdom and strength to assist others in finding their way to freedom.

To be able to offer the deepest possible help, we need to understand how and why we all suffer. This explains why sitting in meditation, or even spending long periods of time in retreat, are acts of compassion. It is only by thoroughly exploring the mechanics of our minds that we come to understand the *real* causes of suffering, to see that we *all* have the potential for liberation and to comprehend how to get there. Then, we can assist others in making those same discoveries.

It is a long-term project, but every time we sit down to meditate, we know there is a great purpose to our lives. We are working on something that will slowly become meaningful on a large scale. This enables us to transcend the feelings of helplessness and despair that often come up when we think about the world situation. Our compassion can now become a strong and dynamic path.

The Buddhist approach views compassion as a trainable skill. If we join our meditation practice with the development of compassion, we now have a project, a plan with purpose. It is important to consider *why* we practise meditation, and to ask ourselves, 'What is my intention? What is it that I want?' Motivation, or intention, is everything.

There is nothing wrong with wanting happiness, but

when we become too obsessed with comfort, we have a problem. There is little chance for any real progress, as we simply remain caught in the habit of grasping, with a feeling that nothing is ever good enough. In Buddhism, we are being invited to have the highest intention: to work at freeing ourselves from all mental limitations, so we can more effectively benefit everyone else. *That* is the vision – total liberation for the sake of all. It puts our lives in perspective, with a powerful sense of direction.

For our compassion to be effective, it has to become unconditional, without an agenda of wanting something back, or even a need to see tangible results. Compassion is less powerful when we are giving help but carrying hidden expectations. This can be debilitating, as we feel discouraged and exhausted when our conditions are not being met. True compassion is limitless and unshakeable.

## HARD TIMES AND COMPASSION

Life's challenges provide us with everything we need. Difficulties take on a new meaning when we discover how to use them to strengthen our compassion, turning those problems into supports for our path. We already have some appreciation of this, as we have all experienced things in the past which felt awful at the time but somehow helped to deepen our character. We know that we have learned something and become stronger.

Hard times can make us more kind. We gain a far better understanding of another's pain when we have walked in their shoes. Perhaps, then, we can feel a sense of gratitude for the difficulties that come into our lives, as they help us to understand the human condition. Challenging as they are, they become the material we need for the growth of our love and compassion.

This attitude is called 'bringing all the obstacles onto the path'. Instead of rejecting whatever we find difficult, it is *all* welcomed into our meditation. We learn how to harness our moments of pain and suffering to enrich our compassion.

Today, there is much discussion about the importance of self-compassion. The best way we can take care of ourselves is by leaning in to our discomfort, rather than resisting it and trying to push it away. If we can master that, then nothing can really hurt us. No matter what happens to us, we *always* have an opportunity to develop our compassion, and don't need to remain trapped in our suffering.

## COMPASSION AND WISDOM

According to Buddhist philosophy, the deepest level of compassion is a recognition that every type of suffering is a problem of perception. If we think that we – and the world around us – truly exist, and that our thoughts and emotions are real, we will suffer. Buddhism and quantum physics agree that nothing is what it seems, and that we are involved in a process of over-solidifying our experiences.

Advanced meditators eventually come to realise that *everything* they experience is a thought, including the so-called objective reality we live in, and that even those thoughts lack any true substance. This causes them to feel the strongest and most profound compassion for the rest of us, as they see how we all get caught up in thinking of things as real. We don't need to get so lost in our pain, as even the worst, most unimaginable distress can always be transformed.

Ultimately, if each of us could look at our situation differently, our suffering would dissolve. The deepest understanding is to know that liberation is possible even in the darkest of times, because the walls of our prison are not solid, but simply made from our thoughts.

## SENDING JOY, RECEIVING PAIN

There is an old Tibetan teaching which says, 'The sacred mystery of life is to exchange self for others.' This points to the heart of compassion training, the practice of *tonglen* or 'sending and receiving'. It is a meditation technique where we imagine taking into ourselves all the pain and suffering of others, and then sending them love, happiness and freedom. That is the exchange.

*Tonglen* creates a revolution in our thinking. It turns our ego-based mentality completely on its head. We mainly tend to focus on ourselves, but that 'me first' approach never actually gives us the happiness we want. By reversing our usual habit, we challenge the ego-centred mind, which can begin to transform through repeated training. Our compassion grows and self-obsession starts to diminish. *Tonglen* reminds us that other people are the cause for any progress we make in our meditation, as it is only because of them that we can cultivate compassion. This makes way for the emergence of a powerful sense of gratitude and love.

In the *tonglen* meditation, as we breathe in, we imagine absorbing into ourselves everyone's suffering from their past, present and future, and sending them joy with our out-breath. It can be helpful to visualise breathing in their unhappiness as heavy, dark smoke and breathing out joy as white light. The process begins with thinking of people to whom we feel close, and then gradually expanding the focus to include others, even 'enemies', and eventually all sentient beings.

It is important to start *tonglen* at a personal level, which is why we usually begin with a friend or relative, otherwise it just remains a vague and theoretical *idea* of compassion. If someone we love were to suffer, we would want to take away all their pain in a heartbeat, if we could.

There is nothing artificial about that type of compassion. It doesn't come from a sense of duty, trying to be noble or a 'goody two-shoes', but it is natural to want to take that person into our arms and remove their pain. It is because we love them, and *that* is the starting point for *tonglen.*

We begin there and then expand the practice out to others, now that our compassion has begun to flow freely. In Buddhist thinking, there is no logical reason why we shouldn't experience the same degree of love and compassion for people we do not know. After all, we have so much in common with them – we all want the same thing, to be happy and free from suffering. Recognising our shared goal creates a sense of affinity.

Our notions of friendship and community are a constantly shifting illusion. Today's best friend might be someone we didn't know a few months or years ago. By that logic, all the strangers we pass on the street are potentially our future friends. Why wait to meet them before feeling close to them? This outlook elevates our compassion and brings greater depth to our practice of *tonglen*.

As our meditation practice develops, we gain a stronger understanding of the human condition. This, too, helps us feel a greater sense of connection, as we realise that we are all in this together. There is less of a feeling of separation, and a deeper appreciation of the hidden pain that people carry within them.

At first, the idea of *tonglen* might feel challenging – why on earth would we want to breathe in toxic smoke? We may wonder, 'Shouldn't it be the other way round? Shouldn't I be breathing out all those nasty toxins and inhaling the white light?' The issue is, the 'other way round' is precisely what creates the problem – it is why we suffer. We have gone through life diligently pushing away discomfort and trying to obtain pleasure, only to become even more controlled by our habits of fear and resistance. This has not worked for us, and never will.

Sometimes it is helpful to start *tonglen* with ourselves. Before going on to do the practice for others, we can spend a few moments moving closer to our own pain. We begin the process by breathing our suffering into our hearts, where it is transformed into joy, and we then breathe that joy back into the places where we have been hurting. This helps us 'lean in' to our fears, so that we can bravely accept and transform them.

*Tonglen* challenges us, but it is perfectly safe. It is a mind-training exercise that creates a fundamental shift in our psychology, a reversal of the ego's normal habits, a fast track to dissolving resistance and expanding our compassion. Eventually, it translates into action, as we become kinder and more giving, with less fear and a stronger ability to help others.

## MEDITATION EXERCISE: *TONGLEN* PRACTICE

Begin your session by sitting with a good posture and spending a few moments establishing the wish to benefit others. This is the compassionate motivation that is the foundation for every meditation.

Mentally count 21 cycles of breath. Breathe naturally, with a complete cycle consisting of an inhalation and exhalation.

Spend a few moments recollecting that everyone, including yourself, has a pure heart buried beneath the rubble of suffering and confusion. All misguided thoughts, emotions and habits are never as solid or tangible as they might seem, but they come and go like clouds in the sky.

Firstly, as preparation, it is beneficial to do some *tonglen* for yourself. Get in touch with your own suffering and discomfort. Breathe in those feelings, taking them into your heart. There, let them be transformed into the light of kindness, and breathe out love, acceptance and compassion into the places where you hold pain. Practise that exchange for a few moments, giving yourself the support you need before going on to think of others.

Now, bring to mind someone you love and care for, perhaps a relative, a friend or even an animal. Alternatively, you could think of someone you don't know, but whose situation powerfully opens your heart. Allow a warm and tender feeling of love to arise, together with a wish to protect them from all forms of pain and suffering. Try to connect with their basic vulnerability, so that your compassion begins to flow.

As you breathe in, imagine that you are taking in all their suffering of the past, present and future, in the form of a thick, dark smoke, which leaves their body and enters yours, dissolving in your heart centre, in the middle of your chest.

As you breathe out, visualise sending them rays of white moonlight, which carry all your joy of the past, present and future, as well as all the happiness and freedom you can possibly imagine. The light of happiness fills them up, bringing them relief and freedom.

Continue to practise that exchange for a few moments, breathing in their pain, and as your heart transforms all their darkness into joy, breathing that joy back into them.

Then, start to extend your circle of compassion. Include the wider group of your friends and family, holding all of them in your awareness as you practise the *tonglen* meditation for them.

Let your focus gradually expand to include acquaintances, then strangers, and finally all beings. You can even include people with whom you have difficulties – nobody is left out.

When you are ready to end the session, let go of the *tonglen* visualisation and spend a few moments resting your mind in a sense of conviction that you and all others have now found deep and lasting freedom. Think that everyone is now filled with the light of wisdom and compassion, free from the causes and conditions of suffering.

• • •

When I first learned *tonglen*, I found the process a little too quick – breathing in suffering, breathing out joy – and it felt a bit mechanical. It was hard to find it meaningful, as I didn't feel there was enough time with each breath. I was then advised to slow down the process by focusing my mind on a few in-breaths in a row, and then a few out-breaths, still breathing in and out evenly. This helped me feel more connected to the practice, and now I find it easier to do it breath by breath.

# CHAPTER 8
# FORGIVENESS

**'The obstacle is the way.'**
**MARCUS AURELIUS**

In the mountains of eastern Tibet, there are monks who enter meditation retreats in remote caves and other wild, desolate places. Sometimes, they will let a local monkey into their cave and then sit quietly in meditation while the monkey runs riot around them. The monkey jumps all over the place, often scratching the meditator's head, sometimes sitting on their shoulder. The monk remains in stillness and equanimity, just letting the monkey play.

There is a long-standing tradition in Buddhism, particularly among the Tibetan schools, of meditators testing themselves by learning to welcome irritations and difficulties without being affected. I am not suggesting we should all lock ourselves in a room with a monkey, but the story illustrates how our obstacles are a matter of perception. When we welcome them as methods for making us stronger, they become like healthy exercise, such as lifting weights in the gym – and the heavier the weights, the more our muscles will grow.

At the heart of Tibetan Buddhism is the practice of *lojong,* which essentially means 'thought transformation'. Its main meditation technique is *tonglen* (which we looked at in the last chapter), one of the most helpful resources we can turn to in hard times. These teachings were first brought from India in the 11th century by the renowned spiritual leader Atisha Dipankara. At the time, Tibet was in a desolate state, as things had fallen apart politically and spiritually. One of the kings of western Tibet had heard about Atisha, and invited him to come to teach and reinvigorate the practice of Buddhism. Atisha received this request and felt inspired to go and help the people of Tibet.

Atisha was known for his ability to use hard times and obstacles as part of his spiritual path. As he began his preparations for the arduous journey, which would involve travelling for many months on foot and horseback across the Himalayas, he had one particular concern. He had heard that the Tibetans were a peaceful and kind people, and he thought to himself, 'Will I learn anything? There will be nobody there to insult me.'

To solve this unusual problem, he decided to take along with him the most difficult person he could find. He heard of a young man who was seeking work and was known to be remarkably bad-tempered, insolent and rude. Atisha paid this individual to travel with him as his assistant, and they journeyed together for several months across the mountains from India to Tibet. They would stop on their way at villages, where Atisha would give teachings. As he was so highly regarded, many people would flock to hear his talks. As the trip went on, some of them would take Atisha aside and say, 'We don't want to interfere, but you are a very famous teacher, and so we are just wondering, couldn't you have got yourself some better staff? Your assistant is a nightmare.'

Atisha would reply, 'He is not my assistant, he is my teacher. He guides me and helps me learn compassion.'

The story goes that Atisha and his grumpy companion became the best of friends, and when they arrived in Tibet, Atisha realised he needn't have brought him along, as there were plenty of difficult people there to work with. It is an amusing story, and one that Tibetans love to tell, of how the compassion teachings came to their country.

The story of Atisha is an example of someone who 'walks the talk', where compassion is not just a theory but a living practice. Atisha possessed a truly open mind and the willingness to learn from anything and anybody. His story exemplifies the complete dropping of resistance and a commitment to finding the deep path to forgiveness in every situation.

## THE POWER OF FORGIVENESS

To build on our compassion training, our next step is to work on forgiveness. Our experiences of compassion are often bound up with limitations and conditions. We can easily catch ourselves thinking, 'After all I've done for them, *how could they*?', which exposes hidden expectations, our sometimes unconscious agenda. We try hard to be kind, but are still operating from the prison of the self, even though we long for an escape.

The freedom we seek will come to us through training, which generally requires a certain degree of resistance, something to work against. Therefore, to speed up our development, it *helps* to have people in our lives who are not always particularly nice to us. They provide that resistance, the chance for us to learn the powerful skill of forgiveness. It is relatively easy to feel compassion for the weak and vulnerable, but when our buttons are pushed, we are challenged to grow. Forgiveness training takes our compassion to a whole new level, by making it complete and unconditional.

We might think of forgiveness as something we do for others, but really, it frees *us*. It allows us to drop our burden of anger. Firstly, we need to own that anger, rather than focusing on the external person or event which triggered us. Then, we can reflect on how forgiveness is necessary for our own emotional wellbeing – we cannot be happy while carrying a feeling of hurt in our hearts. Forgiveness serves us by keeping us connected with our true nature of love, compassion and happiness. Forgiveness is a power, a strength.

It helps to remember that anger and forgiveness cannot exist in our minds at the same time – we can only feel one or the other. Therefore, we can be sure that forgiveness is the best antidote for releasing us from the pain of our anger and upset. We can also see that there is no sound basis for resentment – it is a dead-end way of thinking that lacks reason or understanding. Forgiveness is grounded in a wise outlook. It makes sense, whereas bitterness and resentment do not.

Forgiveness is a skill we can continually work at

cultivating. There are two important aspects to its training, both of which are helpful. One is the path of intelligence and the other the path of wisdom. The first involves using our thoughts in a constructive manner, and the second harnesses the power of our meditation.

## THE PATH OF INTELLIGENCE

The approach here is to celebrate that when we feel hurt, we have been given an opportunity to develop our forgiveness. This does not mean, in any way, that we should condone harmful behaviour, which would simply turn us into a vulnerable 'doormat' and not be good for anyone. On the contrary, forgiveness is a journey to liberation, freeing us from our suffering.

On the path of intelligence we discover a radical form of gratitude, as we can now meet the other person, or our thoughts about them, with a sense of openness and curiosity. Far from allowing them to carry on abusing us, we are grabbing hold of an opportunity to develop our skills. Of course, there are some situations we need to get away from, as they are dangerous and harmful, but once we have done so, we will still benefit from continuing the work of forgiveness.

Essentially, the greater the problem, the more we can learn. The beauty of this attitude is that it creates a shift in outlook. Although we still need to work on ourselves to develop our forgiveness, we are now standing in a very different place, feeling empowered instead of remaining as a victim of hurt.

The next step is to think about the situation from the other person's point of view, rather than only from our side of things. Again, this does not mean to excuse them, but to try to understand the suffering *within them* which has driven their difficult behaviour. Forgiveness involves connecting with the pain in others, and very often, that pain is hidden. It means connecting with the distress that lies beneath a situation.

We often find it hard to forgive, because we assume the other person intended to hurt us. We feel they planned what they did, deliberately, fully out to get us. Sometimes, there was clearly no premeditation, and they lashed out impulsively to harm us. In both situations, we feel hard done by and full of blame. We assume they 'really meant it' or 'should have known better'.

Meditation helps us to dismantle this point of view. In our practice, we begin to see how easily our own thoughts and emotions take over. We become aware of the strong power of our reactive habits and how readily they can control us. We realise that we never *plan* our reactions, and often say or do things which we later regret. In seeing how those reactions come from a place of emotional pain, we can begin to understand that the same is true for others. *Nobody* really 'means it'. No one is actually in control. Even the cold and calculating person is acting from a place of deep confusion and negativity underneath their cruelty. These insights are highly effective in softening the hard edges of our resentment.

We often see things in blunt terms, but walking the path of intelligence gets us to challenge our usual assumptions. Traditional Buddhist texts use the allegory of the stick to illustrate this point. Someone hits us with a stick and we feel angry with them. This is a perfectly normal response, but a deeper analysis can radically transform how we see the situation. We might question why we blame the person rather than the stick – it was the stick, after all, that hit us. Of course, we would counter this by asserting that the stick had no intention or willpower, but was simply wielded by the person. According to that logic, then, why are we not angry with the *anger* in the other person? Surely they are a helpless agent of the rage that is driving them. They are just like the stick, thrown about by their own negativity.

## THE PATH OF WISDOM

While the path of intelligence uses skilful thinking, the path of wisdom lets our meditation do the work. It is helpful to use both approaches on our journey to forgiveness.

We seem to live in an almost constant battle with our minds. When we don't like our thoughts and feelings, we try to push them away. When we do like them, we jump into them, wanting to develop them further. Both approaches are somewhat aggressive in nature, as we are not simply allowing things to be as they are. We constantly want to interfere.

It is easy to see how pushing away troublesome thoughts and emotions is a form of aggression, but it is interesting that the same is also true for those we enjoy: we cannot seem to leave them alone, but often feel a need to build on them. This illustrates a fundamental lack of acceptance. We are telling ourselves we need more – our present state of mind is not alright the way it is. It is as if someone gives us a gift but we tell them it looks too boring and should have been beautifully wrapped, with a shiny bow on top.

Meditation is about leaving things just as they are – there is no need to remove or develop anything. It is a training in complete acceptance and unconditional love – to love something without trying to alter it. It is the essence of the practice of forgiveness. When we can do this with our own thoughts, we can do it with how we see other people.

Everything boils down to a crucial moment that occurs every time we meditate, which is what happens when we realise that our attention has wandered. Many people tense up and experience this as a moment of failure, but actually it is a success – in noticing, we have 'woken up' inside our thoughts and recognised that we got lost. That *is* the meditation.

Instead of attacking ourselves for thinking and feeling, we can accept our minds and leave things in their natural state. In terms of our forgiveness training, this helps us to accept our wounded emotions without stirring them up or suppressing them. Through being known and allowed, they will gradually start to have less power over us. In turn, it becomes easier for us to realise that other people are just as they are, which means we can still love them, even though we might dislike some of their habits and behaviours.

Meditation also helps us to 'merge' with our hurt feelings, as we learned in Chapter Six. Moving closer to our pain, becoming one with it, brings a sense of release and transformation. At a deeper level, it is empowering to realise that we are always greater than our unhappiness. As we connect with our awareness, which is vast, profound and beyond any suffering, we can become more like the deep ocean, undisturbed by its waves.

Again, we are never looking to deny our feelings or to endorse abusive conduct. It is simply that we don't need to feel angry and resentful when we are treated badly. The path of wisdom shows us that we have the power to liberate our minds.

## *TONGLEN* FOR FORGIVENESS

Building on our understanding of the paths of intelligence and wisdom, one of the most powerful practices we can use for developing forgiveness is *tonglen,* or sending and receiving, which we explored in Chapter Seven. It takes on deep significance when we can apply it to our difficult relationships.

In the *tonglen* meditation, we imagine breathing in the other person's suffering and sending them joy with our out-breath. That energetic exchange softens our rage and hurt, as we connect with their story and their suffering, breathing it all deeply into ourselves. We no longer need to feel so afraid of their pain and darkness. We can accept it.

As the mental exchange deepens, a shift will occur. I remember doing this practice quite a bit during my four-year retreat. I would sit on the floor of my little room in the evenings with the lights turned off. I was tormented by thoughts about someone I had felt deeply hurt by over the years. Through patiently doing the *tonglen* meditation, repeatedly breathing in their pain, my own pain and the unhappy dynamics of the entire situation, something in me began to soften.

One evening, during the practice, it dawned on me that the coldness and arrogance I found so difficult in the other person also exists in me, as a form of defence when I feel afraid. I thought, 'Oh. I do that too.' I remember the visceral sense of release this produced in me, allowing me to lay down some of the burden of hurt that had been poisoning me for so many years. I found it incredibly freeing.

You can practise this with current situations, or as 'historical *tonglen*', where you go back to memories of past situations and do *tonglen* for everyone involved. It is important not to push yourself – if you don't feel ready to look at certain things, then that is fine. It is not a good idea to force yourself to open a wound that is not ready to be opened. New feelings of pain might arise while you're doing the practice, and you can also breathe those in, as well as the pain and sadness of all beings. This puts your suffering into a wider context, the human condition. Your own suffering becomes a catalyst for the growth of your compassion. As you breathe out, you are breathing relief and joy into that part of yourself that is hurting, as well as into all the people of the world who are hurting too. The same can also be done if you experience an upsurge of resistance during your practice: 'I can't do this.' In that case, you can breathe in the 'I can't do this' which is in yourself and others, embracing all the resistance and transforming it into freedom on the out-breath.

## MOMENTS OF FORGIVENESS

There is also room for forgiveness training in life's small, seemingly insignificant moments. Just as we did with our 'micro-moments' of mindfulness, we can use the little irritations we inevitably face every day as part of our practice.

Quite often, we struggle with the annoyance of feeling uncomfortable around certain people, finding it hard to accept their quirks or how they behave towards us or others. We might notice how our bodies and minds tense up whenever we see them. The method here is to relax into that tension, meeting it with compassion and a sense of open acceptance. We are being given an opportunity to build our gratitude: this 'annoying' person has shown us where we are stuck, giving us a chance to work on our minds. There are similarities here with our earlier practices of being mindful in queues and traffic jams, where we learned to relax in stressful situations.

Those little moments may seem trivial, but if everyone could learn to transform them, our society today would look very different. Whether we are working with life's minor irritations or major wounds, forgiveness is the key to our freedom, taking us far beyond our limitations and helping us discover unconditional love and compassion.

## MEDITATION EXERCISE: FORGIVENESS

Begin your session by assuming a good posture. Spend some moments establishing a deep wish to benefit others.

Mentally count 21 cycles of breath. Breathe naturally, with a complete cycle consisting of an inhalation and exhalation.

Recollect that everyone, including yourself, has a pure heart and the capacity for inner freedom. We usually cling to our reality as being solid and heavy, but nothing is as tangible as it might seem. That backdrop of non-solidity is an important context for *tonglen* practice.

First, do some *tonglen* for yourself. This means patiently and lovingly breathing in all your feelings of anger and hurt, as a heavy, dark smoke, and then breathing the light of kindness and acceptance into them. Practise this exchange for a few minutes.

Then, call to mind someone you love and care for, such as a relative, a friend or even an animal. Think about them and allow love to arise, with a wish to protect them from every type of pain and suffering. Alternatively, you could think about anyone whose suffering touches you and inspires your compassion.

Now, as you breathe in, imagine that you are taking in all their suffering of the past, present and future, in the form of a thick, dark smoke, which leaves their body and enters yours, dissolving in your heart centre.

As you breathe out, visualise sending them, from your heart, rays of white moonlight, which carry all the joy and happiness you can possibly imagine. The light of happiness fills them up, bringing them relief and freedom.

Continue to practise that exchange for a few moments, breathing in their pain and breathing out joy which infuses every cell of their body.

Then, start to extend the circle of compassion. Include the wider group of your friends and family, and practise the *tonglen* meditation for them too.

Let your focus gradually expand to acquaintances – people you know but don't have a strong relationship with. The essence of *tonglen* is to express the same strength of compassion with each group, without any judgement or discrimination.

The heart of the session is to think of people you have a hard time forgiving, either from now or your past. You could focus on one individual to begin with – someone who has hurt you, or maybe a person you have hurt. It could even be someone from the world stage whom you find it hard to accept or forgive.

Practise *tonglen* with them, deploying the same power of love and compassion that you used in all the previous stages. Breathe in the pain and negativity of that person and send them joy and freedom. Try to feel that you are absorbing the suffering that lies beneath their aggressive words and actions. Then, widen the group to include all your 'enemies'.

Sometimes you might need to pause and again do *tonglen* for your own resentment, breathing it in from within yourself and sending it a sense of relief. Then, include the anger and hurt of all beings.

As the session draws to a close, expand the *tonglen*, now including absolutely everybody.

When you are ready to end your session, let go of the visualisation and spend a few moments resting your mind in a feeling of conviction that you and all others have now been liberated from the causes and conditions of suffering. Everyone is filled up with the comforting light of compassion and wisdom.

# CHAPTER 9
# SICKNESS

**'I wear my sickness as an ornament.'**
**JETSUN MILAREPA**

The Buddha was born as Prince Siddhartha, in the fifth century BCE in India. Soon after the child's birth, an old sage visited the palace and made a prediction that the prince would grow up to be a powerful ruler or a spiritual leader with tremendous impact. He said he would either conquer the world or conquer himself, and things could go either way.

The king was impressed, but felt anxious that the second option might overtake the first, as he wanted his son to become a supreme monarch. As the prince grew, his father became so obsessed by this conflict of paths that he took some highly unusual measures to make sure his child would choose the direction he so strongly desired for him. He felt he needed to keep his son in a bubble where he would be addicted to material life and motivated to attain even more wealth and power.

Siddhartha grew up in a lavish palace without knowing it was actually a prison. Anything he wanted was instantly given to him. His father banned any signs of suffering or decay. Whoever worked there had to be young, healthy and attractive, and even flowers that were wilting were discreetly removed from the gardens by night. The child was brought up in a highly artificial environment, constantly persuaded that material riches provided true happiness and that there was no suffering in the world.

As he grew older, questions began to arise in Siddhartha's mind. He could sense there was something beyond the palace walls he was being kept away from. He eventually managed to sneak out of the gates on four occasions, each of which had a profound effect on him. During these secret journeys, he was accompanied by his loyal attendant, Channa.

On their first trip, they saw an old person bent over a walking stick, moving with difficulty. The boy asked, 'Why are they like that?'

Channa replied, 'Well, they are elderly.'

Siddhartha had no idea that people ever grew old and asked, 'Does that happen to all of us?'

Channa replied that ageing is a natural part of being alive.

This troubled the prince, and he returned to the palace deep in thought. On their second and third forays into the outside world, they saw someone who was clearly very sick, and then a corpse being carried by a funeral procession. They had the same discussion, which again threw Siddhartha into sadness and worry. He had never before been exposed to illness and death.

On the fourth trip, they saw a monk, who seemed completely at peace, radiating a sense of calm. Channa told the prince that this person had renounced worldly life and was on a spiritual path. Siddhartha was struck by this, and went home feeling moved and inspired.

Siddhartha's mind was strongly affected by all that he had seen. He began to question the value of worldly achievements and wonder whether there might be a deeper purpose to our lives. This drove him to abandon his royal home to contemplate these questions, and he entered the jungles and remote valleys of northern India, where he became a meditating monk. In the end, through rigorous practice, he discovered the path that led him to enlightenment and he became known as the Buddha.

One of Buddha's key teachings is that no matter how much we have, we cannot escape the four major challenges of birth, ageing, sickness and death. We need, therefore, to transform our minds, so we can transcend this cycle of suffering, for our own sakes but also to help others do the same. Siddhartha's story is a powerful and relevant metaphor for us today, where our obsession with comfort and wealth has become all-consuming and we try to live in denial of the realities of life and death.

As Siddhartha discovered on his forbidden trips out of the palace, sickness is an inevitable part of life, one that we all have to encounter at a certain point. Whether this comes about due to a temporary illness, or something serious and life-changing, most of us feel unprepared. Even though it sounds counterintuitive, the approach used in meditation is to *move closer* to our suffering, just as we do with other difficult experiences, so that we can dissolve our habits of resistance. This is not easy for us, as we have been brought up in a culture that persuades us that comfort is everything.

## A FRAGILE SOCIETY

We are encouraged to aspire to live just like Siddhartha, in pleasant surroundings shielded from all pain and adversity. The pressure of these expectations means that when we get sick, we assume something has gone terribly wrong and we feel cheated and robbed. We are usually absorbed in the busyness of our daily lives until we are hit by a crisis. Then, we realise just how few internal resources we have for coping with discomfort and hardship. For many of us, our focus has been on seeking happiness from the world around us, and we have given little thought to developing our emotional intelligence or capacity for handling difficulties. When we meet challenges such as illness, we can feel quite helpless as we discover our lack of resilience.

Most of our education systems do not provide us with sufficient skills to help us deal with suffering. Ironically, the emphasis on gathering knowledge and the ingredients for a good material existence hasn't particularly worked for us in terms of providing genuine, stable happiness. Locked in an endless search, we rarely feel fulfilled. Clearly, something does not add up in terms of our priorities and how we define success.

Being part of a Tibetan Buddhist monastery for these

past 30 years, I have found it fascinating to hear a different perspective. Most of my teachers grew up in what was still quite an ancient Tibet. Many of them had never seen a car or encountered electricity, living high above the tree line with no access to fruit or vegetables. Their existence had been rugged and tough, but with a focus on mental and spiritual development.

When the Tibetan lamas first came to the West in the 1960s, they were initially quite surprised and impressed by our level of comfort. They were suddenly exposed to a materially advanced culture and assumed we must all have relatively smooth and easy lives. However, they quickly discovered how emotionally frail we are and just how much we suffer.

They noticed that we all seem to carry a deep sense of vulnerability, constantly at the mercy of what might or might not happen to us. Because we are driven by the belief that all our happiness and misery come from the world around us, we are affected by just about everything. We are told the aim of life is to get as comfortable as possible, but it has made us incredibly fragile, addicted to feeling good and terrified of discomfort. This becomes a major problem whenever we face ill health.

## IMPERMANENCE

Our other issue is a deeply ingrained difficulty in accepting any type of change. We tend to conflate our happiness with obtaining things, telling ourselves we will be happy if we get what we want, and that nothing should ever change or fall apart. The things we latch on to are ephemeral, and so we struggle with impermanence. We are constantly troubled by a feeling that we cannot truly depend on anything or anyone, since nothing lasts, and that we have been putting our trust in the unreliable. At some level we know this to be true, and it scares us, causing us to search for more inventive ways to find security. We go through life feeling incomplete, always sensing that something is missing.

Our battle with change makes it harder for us to cope with sickness. We don't like to acknowledge that our health and bodies are subject to impermanence, and the sense of loss often feels intolerable. We can think we are doomed, unable to imagine an end to our pain and suffering. Again, because we deny impermanence, we don't seem to understand that *everything* changes, including the bad times.

Sickness is challenging because we struggle with discomfort and become limited in our activities, but the deeper issue at play is our profound fear of death. Even when we don't have a life-threatening condition, sickness puts us in touch with our mortality and lack of control. We find it hard to recognise that just as our bodies have come together from various elements, in time they will fall apart. There are very few people who never get sick, but they are still confronted with death, which is inescapable. In that respect, we are *all* terminally ill, and the leading cause of death is life itself.

Our fear of death is reinforced by our denial. We rarely speak about it – culturally, it has become a sanitised topic, one to be avoided. If we were to mention it in daily conversation, we might be thought of as weird and morbid. The fear comes from an avoidance of the truth, where death and impermanence have become dark secrets we would rather not face.

The loss of our loved ones is also extremely difficult. Grief can consume us and leave us devastated. A major factor is the element of shock. Because we suppress our thoughts about it, we feel ambushed and robbed whenever we encounter impermanence – it was 'not supposed to happen' – and the pain can become unbearable. In fact, we struggle with *every* type of loss: our finances, relationships and all the little moment-to-moment 'micro-losses' that we experience every day. The tension comes from our habit of pushing away the inevitable.

Realistically, there is little in life we can be sure of, except that everything changes and each of us will die, with no way of predicting when or how. It is unfortunate that we are so unable to face that one certainty, and that we rarely consider how best to prepare our minds for it. We are locked into our consumer culture with its relentless push for endless youth, impossible standards of beauty and the fantasy of immortality. This outlook comes with the illusion that we can and must live without any degree of discomfort. Therefore, sickness is deeply frightening for us.

## SICKNESS AND MEDITATION

Buddhism doesn't promise magical solutions that will eliminate our illnesses, but instead provides us with methods for mental transformation. If we can work on our minds, there will be tangible benefits in how we experience suffering in our bodies.

For many people, meditation has now become part of a billion-dollar wellness industry, but in those luxury workshops and retreats, there is little mention of impermanence, or of how *wanting* to feel good simply leads to more wanting. The 'wellbeing space' is highly lucrative because, as with any other commercial enterprise, its marketeers know how to make people crave more of their product, keeping the customer hungry.

When we use meditation to enhance our wellbeing, we are subtly telling ourselves we *lack* that wellbeing. When we want something, we are coming from a place of feeling we don't have it. Our quest becomes another endless search, like so many other things in our lives. The wheels of commercialism keep turning, and our meditation practice ends up frustrating and seems fruitless. Hoping to feel better, we attend yet another workshop, and so the chase continues.

The Buddhist approach is to discover that we can be okay with *what is*. Can we be okay with our sickness? Would this make us passive, never reaching for medical help? I don't think so. I think it would help us feel less stressed and upset about our symptoms, more able to handle being unwell and better equipped in making the best choices. It might sound extreme, but in Buddhist philosophy, illness is even considered as a profound opportunity that can open a door to our transformation.

Meditation is the key. It helps us to stop judging our feelings and sensations, which is a particularly important skill for us to learn today, where 'how we feel' has become such an obsession. True healing comes from being comfortable within our minds even when our bodies are falling apart. They will fall apart anyway, when we die, so it is worth thinking about training right now, with acceptance as our focus.

Many people fall into the trap of only doing their meditation when they are in the 'right' mood, but it is good to get into the habit of meditating whenever we are sick, teaching ourselves to stay calm against the odds and to relax our minds when our bodies are struggling. If we can learn to practise when we feel least inclined, we are skilfully training ourselves to stay calm in all situations, and particularly the moment of death.

When someone we love suffers a health crisis or dies, our distress can become immense and overwhelming. Buddhism offers methods which can have a remarkable effect in easing our pain. Using a process of enquiry, we can explore to what extent we actually lose the other person. If everything is ultimately a mental experience, it means that when we think of someone they are here with us, and so we carry them in our hearts even after they have died. Ultimately, is our *thought* about someone really any different from our perception of them when they were physically with us? In both cases, our minds are experiencing our reality.

The next step is to work on transforming our grief and anxiety with the same method we used for other difficult experiences: turning our feelings into meditation by merging with them. We locate the sensations of grief or worry in our bodies, and then relax into the physicality of those feelings, becoming one with them, without resisting or pushing them away. Our grief belongs to the past and worry belongs to the future – they are a narrative in our thoughts, and in this moment there are only sensations. If we can rest compassionately in those sensations, they will begin to transform. This approach allows our experiences of suffering to become much more workable.

If we are practising meditation just to make ourselves feel better, we miss the point, as its strength lies in the cultivation of a deeper wisdom and the resilience we need for handling discomfort with a calm, strong mind. Meditation transforms how we relate to all aspects of suffering, including the challenges of sickness. It teaches us to 'lean in' to our physical discomfort and mental stress, dissolving resistance and becoming comfortable with the uncomfortable.

At a deeper level, meditation practice introduces us to the power of awareness. It can be incredibly helpful to recognise that when we are sick, not every part of us is sick. There is always the watcher or observer, the part that knows we are unwell. Meditation helps us connect with that, allowing us to rest in the spacious freedom of our limitless and expansive awareness.

## SICKNESS AND COMPASSION

Illness becomes fuel for our compassion training when we use methods such as the *tonglen* practice. We imagine breathing in the sickness of others and sending them health and happiness on our out-breath. Naturally, we might wonder if it could be dangerous to 'breathe in' people's sickness, but we should remember this is a meditation practice, aimed at bringing about a shift in attitude, so there is no actual risk to our minds or bodies. Within the relaxed space of meditation, we imagine turning sickness into loving-kindness, like an incinerator burning up suffering. As we do *tonglen*, our state of mind is positive, filled with thoughts of benefitting ourselves and others, which allows the practice to feel helpful and sustainable rather than frightening and unsafe.

If we ourselves are sick, our compassion can become even stronger, as we have first-hand knowledge of the hardships of being unwell. We can use our own physical discomfort as the foundation for doing *tonglen* for the sickness of others, by first applying the practice to ourselves and then turning our attention to everyone else. It is that visceral feeling in our bodies that makes *tonglen* meaningful and personal. Our sickness takes on a deeper significance when it helps us to connect with others.

Instead of feeling destroyed by our health problems, we can think, 'Let me bring all this onto my meditation path. Let me take a firm hold of this illness and allow it to expand my compassion for others, as I now know how they feel.' By cultivating that attitude, we can turn every sickness into meditation.

We can also carry the mentality of *tonglen* into our daily lives, particularly when we encounter anyone who is unwell. Perhaps we could imagine ourselves as their mother. If a mother had a child who became sick, she would want to take on every atom of their pain if doing so would somehow free them. That natural caring instinct is the embodiment of the *tonglen* attitude, the sincere wish to remove the suffering of others. To think of ourselves as everyone's mother builds a sense of compassionate connection.

These methods are exceptionally powerful and might be the most crucial skills we ever learn, especially with our world increasingly telling us that sickness should never happen and that the harsh realities of death and dying ought to be vigorously ignored.

## A BRUSH WITH DEATH

In March 2020, I almost died after catching Covid-19. It was the early days of the coronavirus pandemic, just before the UK went into lockdown. I fell ill while visiting my monastery in Scotland, and immediately entered strict quarantine.

The only available space was an isolated cabin in the monastery grounds called 'the dark retreat house'. It is a small building with no windows, consisting of a 'room within a room', designed for solitary retreats lasting many weeks in complete darkness, an advanced practice for conquering the fear of death.

The building was not being used for such retreats at that time, and there was some light, but it was very dim. This little house became my quarantine cell and sickroom. Monks and nuns from the monastery would kindly leave food outside my door every day, and the abbot would phone me on my mobile to check on me.

The first week was manageable, but on the eighth day, I suddenly got worse. The first sign was that I woke up on the bathroom floor after having passed out. I had a fever of over 40°C and was struggling to breathe. The high temperature persisted, accompanied by extremely laboured breathing. It was difficult to get help, due to the monastery being in a remote area, far from any hospital, and I didn't know what to do. I tried to call the emergency services, but given the national crisis we were in, I was on hold for more than two hours, at which point my phone battery died and I collapsed back into my bed.

Naturally, there was talk of getting me to a hospital, but the nearest facility had informed us that they were completely full. I didn't know whether to call an ambulance that could take me to Glasgow (the closest large city, two hours away), or just to stay put and try to ride things out. I was simply too unwell and confused to think or act with any clarity. Doctors have since told me I was experiencing what is called a cytokine storm, an uncontrollable inflammatory response by the immune system, and that I really should have been hospitalised.

I would spend my days and nights barely able to move, or stumbling between the bed and the bathroom, sometimes sitting in a small armchair, just trying to breathe. Everything was intensified by the sheer claustrophobia of the environment – I was in a house with no windows. I felt trapped inside my feverish body, locked in what felt like a large wooden box.

I was suffering from extremely high fevers which would then break into cold sweats. This went on for some weeks, and I felt fearful of my body and this new, unknown virus, wondering what it might do next. My breathing was so obstructed that I thought I would choke or suffocate. With Covid-19 the lungs sometimes fill up with a hard, sticky phlegm that can block the airways. Not being able to get enough air into one's body is terrifying – how I imagine it must feel to drown. I thought I was dying, and doctors have since confirmed that I was pretty close to it.

It was humbling to discover that even after so many years of being a monk, I was still so affected by fear. It was also a relief to find that I did have internal resources that could help me get through it. I managed to do some meditation, hoping it would help me survive.

I knew I had to shift myself out of the fear, just as I had done in those dark moments during my long retreat and also after Rinpoche's death. Once again, I realised how fortunate I was to have been taught to meditate. I worked on consciously relaxing my difficult breathing, and there were moments when I was able to send feelings of love and compassion into my fear, my symptoms and even into the virus itself. To be angry with the virus – to hate it – only created more suffering in my mind and body. I knew I needed to have compassion for that virus or it would destroy me. Through doing this, my body would relax a little and it became slightly easier to breathe. It is my strong belief that without meditation, I would have died.

The acute sickness lasted a month, and when the fever subsided, I was technically free from the virus, but didn't get much better. I now had long Covid. I eventually managed to see specialists, who confirmed through scans that the virus had caused some damage to my heart and lungs due to myocarditis and blood clots. As I write this, over two years later, I am still unwell with those after-effects.

I am often exhausted, with difficulty breathing and a racing heart. Sometimes my brain feels swollen and inflamed, but I am learning to manage the symptoms, telling myself I'm doing 'research' for this book. There is still uncertainty about recovery time, as so little is known about this novel disease, and most of this book has been written while suffering with long Covid. It has been a rough and difficult journey, but I have learned a lot, and am finally starting to feel a little better.

Again, the only thing that has worked for me during this lengthy period of illness has been to use my symptoms as meditation – embracing them, not pushing them away, but instead, whenever possible, bathing them in a feeling of compassionate acceptance. I am learning to relax into those physical sensations – 'becoming one' with them instead of trying to get rid of them. When I do this, the sharp edges of my suffering become less painful, and I can feel some release. I am grateful, and somehow, the sickness becomes medicine.

### MEDITATION EXERCISE:
### MERGING WITH SICKNESS

This exercise helps you train in resilience by learning how to accept the discomfort of feeling unwell. You can also practise *tonglen*, using sickness as the focus.

Sit on a chair, or lie down if you prefer. Spend a few moments establishing a motivation of compassion – the intention to practise meditation for the benefit of yourself and others.

Firstly, become mindful of your body. Be aware of its contact with the furniture – the chair or bed. Feel the sensation of the weight of your body as it rests on its support.

Trust that your body is safely held and supported – you can let go completely and allow yourself to rest. Notice how subtle micro-tensions in your body have been keeping you 'held up' or 'held together', but you can now release them, as the chair or bed will do the work for you.

Focus on any feelings of physical discomfort and explore the bare nature of those sensations. Try not to label them as 'bad', but simply feel how they feel, without judging them.

When your mind wanders off into distraction, gently bring it back. The physical sensations are your meditation support. Stories about those sensations – all the facts, information and worries about your illness – might take you away, but just keep coming back to the reality of this present moment.

Next, do the practice of 'merging'. Relax as deeply as you can into the discomfort, mentally moving closer to it, as though your mind 'becomes one' with it. Whenever you lose focus, simply return to the process of merging, and go deeper into that sense of connection.

As you become inseparable from your suffering, it might lose its sting, as there is less of a sense of duality, less of a feeling that 'it' is bothering 'you'.

Keep merging until you are ready to end your session, and then conclude with a final thought of compassion, cultivating the wish that your meditation may benefit not only yourself, but all others too.

# CHAPTER 10
# COURAGE

**'In the dark night of the soul,
bright flows the river of the divine.'**

**ST JOHN OF THE CROSS**

St John of the Cross was a 16th-century Spanish mystic who became a monk as a young man and was known for his humility, devotion and fearless courage. He was taken prisoner during the Inquisition, his captors locking him in a tiny cell for nine months. He was starved, given only scraps of food, and was regularly brought out of his isolation only to be brutally beaten. His clothing began to rot and his body became emaciated. Inside that small room, from a desperate and broken place, he began to compose beautiful poems expressing his deep and passionate love for 'the divine'. In the midst of his torment, his mind would enter wildly ecstatic states, after which he wrote down his experiences on pieces of paper smuggled in by one of the guards. He finally managed to escape, and later compiled the verses into his famous work, *La Noche Oscura del Alma* or *The Dark Night of the Soul*. The poignant, radical words of this much-loved text reflect how genuine spiritual awakening can be forged in the darkness of suffering – the breakdown becomes a breakthrough.

Thankfully, most of us are not being imprisoned and tortured, but when we go through hard times, we can certainly feel as if we are locked in a confined space with no room to move or even breathe. We are in a prison of our own minds, feeling suffocated by our thoughts and emotions. The sense of claustrophobia makes us want to do anything to escape – just to get away from our pain – but the path of meditation shows us that solutions can be found within the darkness. For a meditator, hard times are not a problem but a *gift*, where the pain is the catalyst for transformation.

The key to that transformation is to take hold of our suffering and shine the light of meditation onto it, which is only possible if we have first built up a daily habit of mind-training. Without cultivating that mental strength, we become swamped whenever things go wrong. St John of the Cross may have been locked in a cell, but he had his spiritual practice with him, providing all the courage he needed. That prison became the crucible for his alchemy.

Courage is the most essential ingredient on the meditation path. It gives us the ability to maintain our resilience when faced with challenging situations. Courage helps us work with our fears and, ultimately, to transcend them. It also gives us the strength and determination to keep going with our practice, no matter what happens in our lives. There are three key principles in building courage: renunciation, compassion and wisdom. These help us bravely weather the storm when we meet challenges, and they also capture the most important elements of this book.

## RENUNCIATION

Renunciation gives us the courage to stop searching for happiness outside of ourselves, and instead to rely on our own strength. As we begin the meditation journey, our focus shifts from the outer to the inner, we grow less obsessed with the material elements of our lives and learn to start tapping in to our mental power. That change in perspective comes from a wise analysis of where we think happiness and suffering truly come from. If they do indeed come from within us, then it makes sense to put more effort into working on ourselves.

This attitude is known as renunciation. For some people, that word might suggest a harsh form of self-denial and punishing acts of penance. However, renunciation simply means to become comfortable with what *is* and less fixated on acquiring 'things' to make ourselves feel happier. It is a state of total acceptance and complete relaxation into the present moment, regardless of what is happening.

Renunciation means to let go of our old habits and instead to take refuge in the inherent perfection of our own minds. It involves an unshakeable certainty that we can never truly obtain lasting, stable happiness from material objects or other people – we will only ever find it in ourselves. We begin to realise that our suffering has more to do with what happens *in* us rather than *to* us. How we *react* is what defines our experiences, and learning to transform those reactions is the doorway to our ultimate freedom.

Buddha gave his first teaching in the Deer Park at Sarnath, North India, which was at the time a wild and desolate place. His first group of students was a small gathering of friends. He described the pervasive nature of suffering, and how our minds contain everything we need for our liberation. His message was that there will always be hard times, but that they are really a matter of perception, and freedom is always available, deep within us.

Our suffering can wake us up to these truths, a reminder that as long as we keep *looking* for happiness, we will never find it. The suffering itself thus helps to cultivate our renunciation. We start to struggle *less*, as when problems arise, we can remind ourselves that this is just the nature of things, and life is simply doing its job perfectly. The beauty of this approach is that when we accept suffering, it cannot hurt us.

It is helpful to remember that the definition of suffering is '*I don't want to suffer*'. Suffering has no intrinsic reality of its own, but it is a relative concept that depends entirely on its opposite: happiness. It is simply a state of resistance, and ultimately there is *no* suffering separate from the thought of not wanting to suffer.

These key Buddhist principles can make us fearless, with a strong and confident outlook for handling life's difficulties. Engaging with our minds, and working on how we react to our problems, are expressions of true and genuine courage. We become more willing to face ourselves and others compassionately, with a sense of bravery and without trying to block out any discomfort. We know there are answers to be found within our pain, locked in that small, dark space with our fear and suffering.

Are we meditating as a form of escape? It can be tempting to want to 'switch off', or just to experience pleasant sensations, and some modern approaches to ancient disciplines such as meditation and yoga do tend to promise 'finding one's zen', calming down and feeling great. This, however, will always be unsatisfying, as it keeps us caught in a cycle. We can end up suppressing our emotions, until one day they erupt. Our 'zen' is shattered when we leave the yoga studio and start yelling because we discover we have been given a parking ticket. Our meditation practice has not been about real life, but a fantasy of inner peace.

Our happiness will always be unstable when it is bound up with hope and fear. *Wanting* to feel good reinforces our habits of attachment to pleasure and aversion to suffering, and we remain trapped. We often find ourselves *longing* for inner peace, but only in the limited sense of peace and quiet. Some people even seek out peak experiences in their meditation, almost like the adrenaline rush from bungee jumping or taking drugs. None of this can ever satisfy us, as we remain in the cycle of grasping after pleasure and fear of its opposite.

Buddha's teaching on suffering puts everything into context. We don't need to feel so hard on ourselves for going through difficult times – they are a natural part of being alive, and are highly useful for our training. There is no point in rushing around looking for a safe corner where we can be forever happy and never suffer – there is no such corner. We don't need to torment ourselves with trying to solve everything, but we can learn to embrace the present moment just as it is. *That* is the secret path to unshakeable, unconditional joy. We can *always* find that joy, even in the darkness, like St John locked in his prison cell. His body was imprisoned, but never his mind. We too have the power to free our minds.

Consistency is essential. Many people find it difficult to keep up a daily routine of meditation. They feel they *should* be doing it, but don't really want to – other things suddenly seem more pressing and interesting. I went through many years of struggle with my practice: I hated it. What can help us to train more courageously? If we renounce our habit of searching for solutions outside, we can discover how to fall in love with our minds.

Some years ago, I ran into my abbot, Lama Yeshe, in the gardens of the monastery. He had completed his work for the day and was walking up the road to spend the evening meditating in his little retreat house. He seemed excited, telling me he was off to spend time with his best friend and greatest treasure: his mind. His eyes were shining with joy, which I found so inspiring, because at the time, I was finding meditation so difficult. Here was somebody who had discovered the beauty of his own mind. Lama Yeshe has not had an easy life: he was with his brother Akong Rinpoche during their dramatic escape from Tibet, and since then has been plagued by ongoing health problems. Despite all that, he always radiates happiness, which for me embodies the true meaning of renunciation. Instead of being imprisoned by desires and negativity, Lama Yeshe has freed his mind and found real fulfilment.

I am nowhere near his level, but when looking back on those dark times in my four-year retreat, I realise I learned something about transformation, through allowing some of my resistance to drop away. When I discovered how to relax into the suffering created by my emotions, mentally merging with the uncomfortable feelings in my body, the pain would soften and sometimes even melt into sensations of joy. This has given me more courage. I have learned to trust in my mind and have become less afraid of my own thoughts and emotions. I know I have a lot more work to do, but I feel confident that there *is* a way out of suffering, which is to be found by going further *in*.

Meditation is the practice of 'going in'. It helps us to connect positively with our minds and prepares us for life's challenges by cultivating our resilience and courage. That courage can then expand further as we practise small moments of mindfulness throughout the day, renouncing our addiction to distraction and connecting with our own strength. A key ingredient in this is non-judgemental awareness, where we give up our rigid notions of like and dislike, and learn just to be with our experience of the present moment, no matter how that feels and without the usual labels of 'good' or 'bad'. This is the purest form of renunciation, cultivating a level of courage that can carry us powerfully through any of life's challenges.

## COMPASSION

Compassion gives us the courage to meet hard times with openness, rather than shutting down or wanting to escape. We can use *any* difficult situation for our training, allowing some light to shine into the darkness. That light is a feeling of gratitude that our problems, painful as they are, provide us with whatever we need for the development of our compassion. Gratitude creates a strong foundation for the growth of our courage.

The main topic of Chapter Six was how to 'merge' with our suffering and 'become one' with it. This turns us into our own source of compassion. We can learn to love ourselves even when we are in pain, by accepting our experiences wholeheartedly. Instead of feeling desperate for our suffering to go away, we can relax with it, just as it is. That is real courage – the willingness to be with ourselves unconditionally and without resistance.

Through leaning in to our discomfort, we are better equipped to support others, as when we are comfortable with our own pain, we are more ready to face suffering in the world around us, instead of finding it oppressive and frightening. When we discover how to place kindness at the centre of our lives, everything falls into place. Our life's purpose begins to feel more meaningful, with a deeper commitment to be of real benefit. It becomes less of a burden for us to go through some discomfort when that is somehow in the service of compassion, and our meditation practice starts to have a greater sense of direction.

Compassion is the strength to transform pain through making it *useful*. It is the opposite of fear – compassion is powerful courage. Buddhist texts describe the *Bodhisattva*, the meditator with a 'warrior heart of compassion', where true bravery has nothing to do with vanquishing enemies on a battlefield, but a fearless approach to working with our minds and bringing help to others, *no matter what.*

## WISDOM

Wisdom cultivates our insight into the true nature of reality. It is the essence of unshakeable strength and courage, cutting through our delusions and helping us to stop buying into the stories which our minds constantly tell us.

Tibetan meditation texts describe how we 'fight our own shadow', caught up in an almost constant battle with what are ultimately invisible and unreal thoughts and feelings. That war is exhausting, especially if our enemies do not even exist. Everything usually feels so real to us, and we strongly identify with whatever occurs in our minds, assuming there is no way out. Living in that state of fear drains us of all our strength and courage.

The answer is to cultivate our wisdom. In Chapter Five, we explored a process of dismantling our experiences into their various parts. We can identify a mixture of sensations, thoughts, memories, reactions, etc. There are many components, showing us that nothing is as concrete and singular as we might have assumed. For example, the experience of physical pain requires a body, pain and awareness; it also requires a habit of disliking discomfort. There are several moving, shifting elements. Our suffering will begin to disintegrate when we stop giving it a solid, unchangeable identity.

It is important to remember that whenever we suffer, not every part of us is in pain. There is always a watcher or observer. How do we know we are suffering? The knower does not suffer – it is observing the discomfort. The sky is always bigger than its clouds, and the ocean is deeper than its waves. Similarly, our awareness is never unhappy. This outlook is the epitome of fearlessness: the observer can never be hurt.

Buddhist philosophy is radical and cutting edge, blowing apart our habitual patterns of perception and getting us to question the very fabric of our reality. It encourages a deep investigation into the nature of our experiences, through a precise examination of our minds. The origin of these methods, the Buddha, is not just a statue in a temple, but a symbol of our intrinsic wisdom, our potential for awakening. Buddha is a constant source of courage as we realise that no matter what goes wrong in our lives, nothing can ever damage our true nature.

We are all here to wake up. Every human being has an in-built, natural aptitude for awakening – neuroscientists identified what they called the 'god spot' in the brain, an area primed for spiritual experience. Other experts have since discovered that the brain has not just one, but *many* such regions, which is even better news. Buddhists would say that we *all* have a drive towards freedom and awakening, because that is who we truly are. Everything we do points in that direction, even when we are lost in desire, which only means we are looking for our freedom in the wrong places.

It is empowering to acknowledge that, essentially, our minds contain all the happiness we have been searching for. Our culture seems to keep us locked in a state of unfulfilment, unable to recognise our own perfection. We can often feel there is something lacking in us and that we need to be rescued. The Buddhist teachings show us how to free ourselves, and that each of us possesses fundamental, original goodness. We are all crystals, covered in a layer of mud.

Our mud might be heavy and thick, or just a thin coating, but it can always be cleaned away, revealing the crystal which was always there. To meditate is to clean the mud. Deep down, we are all free from suffering. Deep down, there is absolutely nothing wrong with any of us.

## MEDITATION EXERCISE: COURAGE

This exercise contains several elements that help to culti-vate courage.

Sit with a good posture. Spend a few moments estab-lishing a motivation of compassion – the wish to practise meditation for the benefit of yourself and others.

Be mindful of your body. Become aware of its contact with the chair. Sense those points of connection and relax into the feeling of the weight of your body.

Next, focus on your breathing. Breathe through your nose if you can, and try not to alter the breath – just allow it to remain natural. Follow the air with your mind, as it comes in and out of your body. When your attention wanders, gently bring it back to the breath. Do this for a few moments.

The next step is to acknowledge that everyone, including yourself, has a pure heart buried under all the stress, like the crystal covered by mud. It is also helpful to remember that all confused thoughts and emotions are not solid or tangible, but they come and go like clouds in the sky.

Visualise that inside the centre of your chest, there is a glowing ball of white or pink light. Imagine that this light represents the inherent purity and goodness of your deepest, most compassionate nature. Spend a few moments resting in the feelings of loving-kindness that emanate from the ball of light within you.

Next, practise *tonglen*, first using your own suffering as the focus. Pay attention to where in your body you feel uncomfortable. Perhaps it is one area, or several. It could even be your whole body. Make a heartfelt wish that through your experience of this discomfort, you may free others.

Breathe your suffering into the ball of light, where it is transformed into a feeling of deep happiness. This is then breathed into the place in your body where you feel stuck. You can use the visualisation of dark smoke on your in-breath, and white light on your out-breath.

Then, think about someone who you know is suffering, and do *tonglen* for them. Imagine that you breathe in all their problems, in the form of a heavy, thick smoke that leaves their body and enters yours. The smoke is completely absorbed into the ball of light in your chest, where it is transformed by the power of compassion into rays of light, just like moonlight.

Those light rays emanate from you and shine into the other person, filling them with happiness. Continue with this exchange for a couple of minutes.

The next step is to widen the focus. Think of others and extend the *tonglen* to them. Begin with people you know, and then gradually expand it to all beings, including those you have problems with.

Then, let go of the *tonglen* meditation, and focus again on the ball of light inside your chest. Imagine that it gently radiates light into every part of your body, filling you with feelings of joy, happiness and freedom.

Finally, imagine that your entire body is made of light, which slowly begins to dissolve into emptiness, so that nothing is left but your perception of a vast and limitless space. Rest your mind in that sense of expansiveness for a few moments, and then end the session.

As always, finish your session by making a mental commitment to the happiness and freedom of yourself and all others, knowing that this is the reason why you meditate.

# ACKNOWLEDGEMENTS

I owe everything to my spiritual teachers Chöje Akong Tulku Rinpoche and Lama Yeshe Rinpoche, as well as my parents, Indira and Ben.

As always, I would like to thank my wonderful publisher Liz Gough at Yellow Kite, whose kindness, patience and insight have helped to nurture me and bring this book to fruition.

I also want to thank my brilliant editor Imogen Fortes for her skill and clarity, and I am grateful to Sara Sjölund for her expert help with structure and editorial guidance. Huge thanks also to Allegra Wint for helping me with the final edits.

Ruby Wax and Ash Ranpura, your friendship and kindness are everything. I also offer my love and gratitude to Ani Tselha, Lorraine and Anthony Harris, Elizabeth Seetal and Catherine Brown, as well as all who have supported our meditation centres.

Thank you also to my excellent and kind admin team, Emily Field, David Cushion and Sauba Habib, and to all the wonderful people who have attended talks over the years and asked such insightful questions.

# MORE MEDITATIONS

## BODY SCAN

This meditation exercise helps with relaxation. You are going to move your focus slowly down through your body, like a scanner that observes each section: front, back, middle and sides.

Sit in a comfortable chair or lie on your back on your bed or the floor, with your spine straight. If you are lying down, it helps to put a pillow or cushion under your head for support. You could also place another pillow under your knees.

Begin your session by spending some moments cultivating a compassionate motivation. Mentally set the intention that you are going to meditate for your own benefit and the benefit of all others.

Firstly, feel the contact between your body and the chair, bed or floor. Get a sense of the heaviness of your body, as well as its stillness.

Then, focus your attention at the top of your head for a few moments. Next, let your awareness travel down to your forehead. Steadily move the focus to your eyebrows, then your eyes, ears, cheeks and nose.

Next is your mouth – lips, teeth and tongue. Then, become aware of your jaw, the back of your head and neck. Shine the light of your awareness into all those areas, one after the other.

Focus on the tops of your shoulders, then move your awareness down to your armpits. It is common to feel some tension in the shoulders, but try to remain neutral, not judging or labelling, just leaving things as they are.

Next, move down your arms: to your elbows and forearms, wrists and hands, and then all the way to your fingertips.

Throughout this process, your mind will keep drifting away. When you realise you have become distracted, simply bring your attention back to the area you had been focusing on, gently returning and using your body as the anchor.

Take your awareness back up to your shoulders, and begin to travel down your torso, taking in all areas of the front, sides, spine and inside, level by level.

Next is your lower abdomen, waist and then your hips. After that, focus on your buttocks, pelvis, groin and then thighs. Paying attention to both legs at the same time, travel down to your knees, and then further down the legs into your ankles.

Finally, focus on your feet, starting with your heels, then moving from the soles to the tops, and then all the way to the ends of your toes.

Simply feel whatever you feel or don't feel, without adding too many labels or judgements.

You're not *trying* to feel anything. In some places, there might be strong sensations, such as pain or tension, but in other places, you won't necessarily feel a thing. That is fine – just experience your body as it is in this moment, without too much mental conversation about it. Allow yourself to relax naturally, rather than trying to *push* yourself into a relaxed state.

The final step is to be present with your whole body, noticing its weight and stillness. Feel its contact with the chair, bed or floor.

Then, become aware of the gentle movement of your breath. Breathe naturally and feel how your body subtly rises and falls with each inhalation and exhalation.

Finally, to end your session, think again of the motivation of loving-kindness and compassion, reminding yourself that you are meditating for the benefit of all.

## COUNTING THE BREATHS

This is a good meditation for times when your mind feels very busy or scattered. Counting can give you a stronger and more tangible focus.

Find a quiet place and sit on a chair, with a good posture. Breathe through your nose if you can, otherwise through your mouth.

Mentally set the intention of kindness. Spend a few moments cultivating the motivation that your practice is for your benefit and the benefit of others: as you progress on your journey, your ability to help yourself and others find liberation from the root causes of suffering will expand and grow.

Firstly, feel the ground under your feet, and then pay attention to where your body is in contact with the chair. Shift your awareness to the feeling of the texture of the clothing under your hands, which are resting in your lap or on your legs, and then focus on your shoulders. Be aware of your face, allowing its muscles to relax, and then the front of your body, your abdomen. Spend a few moments on each of these areas.

Notice how your breath gently moves your body with a subtle contraction and expansion. You might sense this in your abdomen or your chest. Remember to breathe naturally and without effort, not trying to breathe deeply, but just allowing the breath to be as it is.

Your mind will wander, but when you notice that has happened, gently come back to your breath, again and again.

This is the main step, so spend most of the session here: mentally count your breaths, with the complete cycle of the in-breath and out-breath as one number. Again, remember to breathe naturally and without effort: these are not deep-breathing exercises. Try to count up to seven cycles, and then return to number one and start again. Whenever you lose count, it simply means your mind has wandered, so start again from the beginning, without getting tense or feeling any sense of failure.

When you become stronger at counting without losing focus, you could extend the goal to 21 cycles, repeated as many times as you wish.

To end your session, focus again on your body for a few moments. Feel its contact with the chair, and then sense the ground under your feet.

The last step is another moment of compassion, remembering that you are training in developing greater kindness towards yourself and others, as a path to complete freedom.

## SOUND MEDITATION

This practice can be useful if you are somewhere noisy, but it can also be done anywhere, as there will always be subtle sounds in your environment.

Sit with a good posture, or if you are doing this meditation in a busy place, sit in whatever way feels the most balanced and comfortable.

Set the intention of compassion, remembering that you are meditating for your own benefit and the benefit of all others.

Become aware of your body. Feel its contact with the chair or the floor, and then focus on your shoulders, face, arms and then hands.

Turn your attention to whatever sounds you can hear, without trying to separate them out, identify or label them. Simply hear whatever you are hearing, as if for the very first time.

Be present with the sounds, allowing them to keep you in the here and now, without judging any of them as 'good' or 'bad'. The noises might be loud, or quite subtle. Your ears are hearing, and so too is your awareness.

When you notice that your mind has wandered, just come back to the bare reality of experiencing this moment, using sounds as your anchor.

To end the session, focus on your body for a few moments, and then remind yourself of the intention of kindness and compassion.

## RIVER MEDITATION

This practice can be helpful when you are feeling stressed, afraid or emotionally stirred up. It is done either sitting next to a river or a stream, or imagining one in your mind's eye.

Begin your session by establishing the heartfelt wish to benefit yourself and others. This is your compassionate motivation for meditation.

Look at the river, or imagine it, and try to get a sense of its movement and flow. If you focus on one part of the water too tightly, you will become tense or perhaps even a little dizzy. It is best to be aware of the general flow. As you do this, try to feel that your mind is just like the river, gently moving and not solid. Your thoughts and feelings, particularly any that are stressful, are just part of the water, and you don't need to hold on to them – let them flow with the river.

This meditation also helps you gain a deeper appreciation of impermanence. As you look at the water and think, 'This is a river,' the part you are looking at and identifying as the river has already flowed away. All things are like that: constantly changing and never static or permanent.

Use the flow of the water to help you cling less to the seeming solidity of your thoughts, feelings and experiences. Allow them to travel in the water, letting go of your tight hold on them.

To end your session, spend a few moments focusing on your body, feeling the ground under you, relaxing your shoulders and paying attention to your breathing.

Conclude with another moment of compassion, by mentally dedicating your session to the happiness of all.

## HAPPINESS AND SUFFERING

This is a contemplative practice, which means using your thinking mind to analyse and reflect upon a theme. The topic is the nature of happiness and suffering, exploring their origin and how best to work with them. The aim of the practice is to increase your sense of enthusiasm for the path of meditation, encouraging you to become more diligent.

Begin your session by sitting with a good posture and reminding yourself of the compassionate intention for meditating – you are doing this for your own benefit as well as for others.

Be aware of your body for a few moments, and then focus on your breathing. Count 21 cycles of breath, remembering to breathe naturally.

Then, think about the nature of happiness. Ask yourself: what is happiness and where does it come from? Does it come from the world outside, or is it ultimately more of an internal process?

Try to ask these questions from a place of quiet reflection, calmly and incisively contemplating the topic at hand.

Then, let go of that and do 21 more cycles of breathing.

The next step is to think about the nature of suffering. Ask yourself a series of questions: what is suffering? What are its causes and are they external or internal? See what answers come up, and reflect on them.

Again, do 21 cycles of breathing.

The last contemplation is on the nature of freedom. What is genuine freedom, and how can you get there? What role does your meditation practice have in that process?

End your session by relaxing, being aware of your body for a few moments. Then just sit and let your thoughts come and go like clouds in the sky.

The final step, as always, is to mentally dedicate your practice to the benefit of all, including yourself.

## INNER COMPASSION MEDITATION

This helps you connect with your potential for awakened compassion. It can also be a good meditation to do before the start of a *tonglen* session.

Sit with a good posture, upright and with a straight back. Generate a deep wish that your meditation practice will help you to benefit not only yourself, but all others too.

Be aware of your body. Feel its contact with the cushion or chair under you, and feel the ground beneath your feet. Be aware of your shoulders, then your face, followed by your abdomen.

Count 21 cycles of breath.

Next, visualise a golden sphere of light resting upon an open lotus flower that sits horizontally in the space just above your head. Imagine that the ball of light represents awakened, limitless, unconditional compassion. Mentally reach out to it, with a sense of longing to become one with it, sincerely wishing for the qualities of love, compassion and wisdom to awaken in your heart.

Imagine that the ball of light on its flower seat now slowly descends and enters the crown of your head. You are not solid, but transparent, also made of light. The light sphere travels down inside your body to the centre of your chest, at the level of your heart. It rests there, on its open lotus flower.

Try to feel a sense of inseparability with the light. As it becomes part of you, it illuminates the hidden depths of your own compassion. Rest your mind in the feeling of confidence that all the qualities of limitless, unconditional love are intrinsic to you.

Spend some time meditating on that, focusing your mind on the image of the ball of light inside you, with a feeling of unity and peace, knowing that your mind and the power of compassion have mixed together and become as one.

When you are ready to end your session, make a deep wish that you will benefit others through your compassion.

## LOVING-KINDNESS MEDITATION

This practice develops your loving-kindness. It is traditionally known as *metta* practice.

Sit with a good posture. Generate the motivation to practise for the benefit of all.

Become aware of your body, feeling its contact with the chair, and then become aware of your shoulders and face. Next, feel the ground under your feet, just for a few moments.

Visualise that in the centre of your chest, there is a glowing ball of white light, slightly tinged with the colour pink. Feel that this light sphere represents all the love and compassion of the deepest aspect of your mind.

Imagine that it glows and emanates rays of light that slowly fill your body. Feel as if you are being bathed in love, kindness and happiness from within, and that all your stress and suffering begin to dissolve away. Deep in your heart, cultivate a wish that you may be happy and free from suffering.

The rays of light then spread from your body, reaching out to others. Begin by thinking of someone you feel close to, and send the light rays to them, offering them love and kindness. Imagine the light fills them and melts away all their problems. At the same time, generate a sincere wish for them to be well and to have happiness and peace.

Now, extend that wish to your family and friends, and allow the light to radiate from the sphere in your heart. It fills them completely, while you make the same wish for their happiness.

Then, think of strangers and even 'enemies' in the same way, with the intention that they may achieve total happiness.

Spend a few minutes on each step, and then wish for complete happiness and freedom from suffering, for absolutely everyone. The rays of light are now flooding the entire world, even the universe, with loving-kindness.

To end your session, let go of the visualisation of light and spend a few moments relaxing your mind with a feeling of kindness and freedom.

## FORGIVENESS PRACTICE

This exercise begins with doing some writing.

Think about someone you are struggling to forgive. Another option would be to think of someone who has issues with you.

Using pen and paper, write a letter to them, in which you describe exactly what they did or said, how you feel about what happened, and what you think of them. Don't hold back: just let it all out and be as honest and true to your feelings as you can. You are not actually going to send the letter, so you can let rip!

Once you have completed it, read through the letter. Don't judge any of your feelings as you read, but simply allow the emotions to be as they are.

The next step is to write a letter to yourself, writing as if you are that person. Write about the situation from their point of view, describing what happened, what they were feeling and how it affected or didn't affect them. Again, once the letter is written, read it to yourself.

Notice any feelings that come up as you read, allowing them just to be, without judging.

The third letter to write is from a neutral person, somebody outside the situation. You can simply invent someone – it doesn't need to be a real individual. This letter is not written to either of you, but is instead more like a statement.

Write as that person, dispassionately, about what has happened between the two parties. Afterwards, read the letter back to yourself.

It can be illuminating to become aware of those three different perspectives – yours, the other person's and the neutral third party's. This can help to melt any rigid perspective you might be holding on to, and it becomes the gateway to forgiveness.

Now, you are ready to do some meditation practice. Sit comfortably with a good posture. Spend a moment establishing your motivation of loving-kindness and compassion, a deep wish that you may help yourself and all others find happiness and freedom.

Be aware of the room around you, and then feel the contact between your body and the furniture.

Focus on your breathing for a short while, remembering to breathe naturally and without any pressure.

Then, imagine that the person to whom you wrote the letter is now sitting in front of you, facing you.

As you breathe in, think that you are taking in all of their thoughts and feelings, as well as their happiness and suffering – in fact, their entire personality. Breathe it all into you.

As you breathe out, imagine that you send them all your thoughts, feelings and personality. All of that enters them.

If it is difficult to do the exchange breath-for-breath, then focus mainly on your in-breath a few times, and then your out-breath.

Continue with the process until you feel there has been a full and complete exchange.

Now, try to sense how the other person feels. All their emotions are now within you, so try to understand their pain, their suffering – all the things that have been driving their behaviour.

Also, because of the exchange that has taken place, you have let them know how you feel, since they now have all your thoughts and emotions inside them.

Spend some time simply feeling how they feel, inhabiting their inner world, which is now inside you. Try to offer some acceptance and compassion to those emotions, with a sense of openness and an absence of judgement.

Where are your hurt and resentment now? You have sent them into the other person, so you no longer feel them in you.

Finally, bring your own feelings back into yourself, but keep the other person's there within you, too. Relax with all of that, and with a sense of compassion for both of you.

Relax even more deeply, allowing your mind simply to be present. Let your thoughts and emotions pass by like clouds in the sky, trying not to grab on to them.

End your session by making a heartfelt wish that you, the other person and all others in the world will find freedom from hurt, resentment and suffering, as well as the achievement of stable happiness and freedom.

## SICKNESS MEDITATION

Sit with a good posture and establish the motivation of compassion, the wish to practise meditation for your own benefit and that of others. If you are too unwell to sit upright, it is fine to do this practice lying down.

Be aware of your body, feeling its contact with your seat or bed.

Spend a few moments meditating on your breathing, naturally and without effort. When your mind wanders, keep returning to the breath.

Pay attention to the place in your body where you experience the strongest pain, discomfort or illness. If you feel unwell in many places or in your entire body, try to identify an area where you are suffering the most. If it is too much for you, don't push yourself, just go back to your breathing until you are ready.

Inside the area of sickness and discomfort, visualise a small sphere of light, either white, blue or pink – whichever colour feels the most healing for you.

Think that the ball of light contains all the healing powers of your true inner potential, your 'Buddha mind'. Visualise it in the centre of the place where you feel unwell, and that it starts to emanate a pure, healing nectar, which fills up the area of sickness. Imagine that this nectar has a liquid nature, with the power to liberate you from your pain.

As the nectar fills up that area, your body begins to feel safe, and you can deeply relax.

Then, imagine that the nectar spreads throughout your body, gently and gradually. As it does so, your body becomes even more relaxed, healthy and at ease.

Visualise that your entire body is now filled with the nectar, and any traces of suffering have been washed away.

Your body is filled with the pure, healing liquid of compassion. Now let go of the visualisation and just rest your mind in the present moment, allowing thoughts and emotions to come and go like clouds in the sky.

If you wish, you can then imagine the same process happening for others, using the visualisation of the ball of light in the parts of their bodies where they feel unwell.

End your session with a few moments of sensing the chair, floor or bed under your body and gently being aware of your breathing.

Finally, make a heartfelt wish that you and all others may be free from the sufferings of sickness and pain. May everyone find the strength to be at peace, even when challenged by illness and hard times.

Also by Gelong Thubten

# A MONK'S GUIDE TO HAPPINESS: MEDITATION IN THE 21ST CENTURY

Paperback ISBN 978 1 473 69668 6

We are all on a quest for happiness,
but we tend to look in the wrong places.

We look externally to find contentment, thinking
that material possessions will give us what we want.
*A Monk's Guide to Happiness* explains how and
why we need to search within, and connect with our
essence, in order to find true peace and freedom.
Everyone has the potential to be happy, as we are all
'hardwired' for happiness.

How do we get there? By meditating. Not just in
the morning, but throughout the day by introducing
micro-moments so we never drop the mindfulness ball,
even when we're busy. Meditation is more than just
a stress-reduction tool or a relaxation therapy, but
the key to finding long-lasting, sustainable happiness. It is
also a way to bring more compassion into our hectic,
modern world.

books to help you live a good life

Join the conversation and tell
us how you live a #goodlife

🐦 @yellowkitebooks
📘 YellowKiteBooks
📌 Yellow Kite Books
📷 YellowKiteBooks